COLOR
OUTSIDE
the LINES

SWINDOLL
LEADERSHIP
LIBRARY

COLOR OUTSIDE the LINES

A Revolutionary
Approach to
Creative Leadership

HOWARD G. HENDRICKS

CHARLES R. SWINDOLL, GENERAL EDITOR

WORD PUBLISHING

NASHVILLE

A Thomas Nelson Company

COLOR OUTSIDE THE LINES
Swindoll Leadership Library

Published in association with Dallas Theological Seminary (DTS):
General Editor: Charles Swindoll
Managing Editor: Roy B. Zuck
The theological opinions expressed by the author are not necessarily the
official position of Dallas Theological Seminary.

Hendricks, Howard G.
Color outside the lines : learning the art of creativity / by Howard Hendricks.
p.   cm.—(Swindoll leadership library)
Includes bibliographical references.

ISBN 0-8499-1365-9

1. Creative ability—Religious aspects—Christianity. I. Title. II. Series.

BT709.5.H46   1998
248.4—dc21   98-26781
                                                                CIP

Printed in the United States of America
98 99 00 01 02 03 04 05 06 BVG 9 8 7 6 5 4 3 2 1

Contents

Foreword

You want creativity? I'll give you creativity in two words: Howard Hendricks!

In a day when Christians tragically mistrust artists and minimize esthetic value, I find it refreshing that a seasoned scholar, teacher, and Bible expositor has written a volume linking effective biblical ministry with *creativity*. Talk about a book that's overdue!

In vintage Hendricks style, my esteemed mentor and longtime friend, with lighthearted ease, helps us bulldoze away the crusted layers of dull thinking that have settled in our minds like green-brown slime at the bottom of a country pond. He refuses to let all that stuff sit, soak, and sour.

He challenges us to see life and ministry through a different perspective. To go beyond what is comfortable and predictable and reach for a level of imagination that compels and inspires people to respond. And since we are talking about communicating the glorious life-changing message of Christ, his mandate for fresh, creative approaches to proclaiming the Good News rings loud and clear.

As always, Dr. Hendricks has done his homework. This volume is not the result of a frustrated, preoccupied theologian trying hard to connect. He is grounded in the Scriptures and brings to this subject years of not only teaching creativity, but also *doing* creative teaching. This is one man who truly "practices what he preaches"—every time!

I commend this book to pastors, teachers, evangelists, missionaries, public speakers, small-group leaders, Sunday-school teachers, and anyone else wishing to impact the lives of people whom the Lord has called you to serve. In my opinion, the number-one tragedy in Christian education today—despite all the advances in technology and creative arts—is a teacher who is boring! This volume is a sure cure for that common pedagogical disease.

Here is your opportunity to be schooled by the master communicator on how to think creatively as well as how to be creative. You may be surprised just how wonderful a picture God creates in your life and ministry when you allow yourself the freedom to "color outside the lines."

Happy coloring!

—CHARLES R. SWINDOLL
General Editor

Preface

Everyone is born a genius, but the
process of living de-geniuses them.

—R. BUCKMINSTER FULLER

Like a verbal bombshell, the word *creativity* explodes shrapnel into the private wish list of most people. This is because we have stuck the label on a few artistic super-achievers and envy it as a touch of genius—out of reach for most of us mortals.

Today the "new and different" has achieved a dizzying popularity. Creativity has dilated into "more than a word today; it is an incantation . . . a kind of psychic wonder drug, powerful and presumably painless. Everyone wants a prescription," says John Gardner,[1] with his uncommon perception of our human quest for elixirs.

As Christians, of course, we want to be inventive and original. But our efforts often send eyeballs rolling and bosses shaking their heads benignly as if we were village idiots. We privately agree with the kids that the worship service, the Sunday-school class, or the youth group is pretty boring. And we long to present the gospel message more attractively. But how?

Like icons on a computer screen, creativity evokes pictures in our heads: Disneyland, cartoons, or some famous performer. Perhaps *Alice in Wonderland*, the *Iliad*, a symphony, or a famous painting illustrates for us invention and new expression.

We all recognize that artists, actors, and inventors are creative. Perhaps we think of an eccentric uncle who writes weird poetry, a cousin who concocts unheard-of games, or a next-door neighbor whose home is unusually unique. Yet few of us feel that creativity defines our own efforts. We strive to be individualists but often find ourselves merely imitating others. How, then, can we become creative?

Beautiful blooms always grow out of fertile soil. Ink on paper can never give birth to your own vision and inspiration, but it can jump-start your thinking and fuel your possibilities. Eric Hoffer, the famous blue-collar union worker who became a writer/motivator, has defined creativity as "discontent translated into art." That's my hope for you—that this book will inspire a holy discontent that propels you to get up and go! I yearn for every reader to find here a resourceful environment from which he can develop a can-do lifestyle.

Young people often ask me, "Should I go to seminary?" I respond to their question with a question of my own: "What do you want seminary to do for you?"

"Oh," an eager prospect replies, "I want to be a man (or woman) of God!" Fantastic! But the brutal fact is, no seminary or any other institution can make you a man or woman of God. Hopefully it can motivate and equip you, but only God can make you to be like Himself. You will be as spiritual as you are willing to trust Him to make you.

So it is with creativity.

When man in Eden first turned away from the One who created him, he began a journey that would take him steadily away from his divine Designer. Drudgery sank into boredom and sagged into rebellion and violence. Had not the loving Father intervened with His most creative solution—Jesus Christ, God in the flesh—mankind would have destroyed itself.

Imitating our God and Savior allows us to reverse the downward trend, to conceive new ideas and formulate fresh approaches to life and ministry. I invite you to join me in a page-turning seminar that could overthrow the stale and sterile government of your thinking.

What is it, this something that exists in select people to make them clearly originals? Is it a genetic spin that God drops into families? A state of mind that happens in certain rare environments? Why does creative thinking seem so easy for some but totally elusive for others? How can many people be so boringly predictable, while others always seem to be ambushing from an exciting and unexpected direction?

When the governor of North Carolina complimented Thomas Edison on his inventive genius, Edison denied that he was a great inventor. "But you have over a thousand patents to your credit, haven't you?" asked the governor. "Yes," replied Edison, "but my only original invention is the phonograph. I guess I'm an awfully good sponge. I absorb ideas from every source I can, put them to practical use, and improve on them until they become of some value. The ideas are mostly those of others who don't develop them themselves."[2]

Edison's words provide a clue to our discomfort with the idea of our own latent creative ability. His key words: "ideas," "improve," and "value."

Every one of us is born with a unique human capability to think independently and then to evaluate and implement our thoughts into constructive productivity. Of all the creatures God made during those dazzling days of creation, only one had the ability to produce surprises. Only one couple was given free will to think voluntarily in areas apart from what they already knew. All other life is subject to the laws of nature, totally predictable. One has only to learn the distinctive attributes of a particular beast in a given environment to anticipate the appropriate and probable behavior.

Not so with God's culminating handiwork. Humanity stood alone in the image of the Maker, totally free to make his and her own decisions. Only human beings are capable of improbability, of independent judgment, and of behavior beyond ordinary expectations. "The reason kids don't have to be taught to be creative is that creativity is essential for human survival. Virtually every other species in the animal kingdom is born with a fully formed repertoire of reflexes and responses. Not so the human; we alone must learn and master from scratch almost everything we need to know to survive."[3]

No form of illiteracy in contemporary America is as widespread and costly as our ignorance of history and the creative process. Listen to Norman Cousins, a thoughtful commentator. "One of the unhappy characteristics of modern man is that he lives in a state of historical disconnection. . . . The past has nothing of value to say to us. . . . Into a few decades have been compressed more change, more thrust, more tossing about of men's souls and gizzards than have been spaced out over most of the human chronicle until then. . . . The metabolism of history has gone berserk. . . . The soul of man has become septic."[4]

The past, said Cousins elsewhere, is dead only for those who lack a desire to bring it to life and to profit from its lessons. To the progenitors of the "now" generation, disregard for the past was no problem. But their generation had not yet been battered and confounded by acceleration. We must believe today that history has much of value to say to us, who are like tumbleweeds spinning out of control across a West Texas prairie. When we are desensitized to the world around us, we are also numb to the opportunities and possibilities before us.

Whatever a person's lifestyle, creativity is within reach. The purpose of this book is to help unlock the reservoir of untapped possibilities for every reader. Christians, those who have responded to the divine message of life through Jesus Christ, have everything they need to be eminently creative. We not only have a message; we also have a mission to communicate good news to a world parched with ordinariness and empty experiences. Ease and predictability are not among God's promises to His children. It is my prayer that you will never think the same way again after having pondered these pages.

Christians have limitless capacities for growth, but it requires an explosion of the imagination. No one is beyond the scope of creative thought. For all of us, our brains are repositories of far greater potential than we have ever dreamed—if we learn to access it.

Since our present-day world fosters a confused and disorderly habitat, most of us tend to pick up a prosaic and barren lifestyle, a daily grind that inspires little. Yet it was precisely confusion and chaos that occasioned many great deeds. Dante's *Divine Comedy* came as a result of watching a boiling cauldron of smelly tar. William Booth conceived the idea for the Salvation Army as he walked through a reeking and hopeless-looking slum in nineteenth-century London. Lewis Carroll is said to have designed much of his *Alice in Wonderland* while suffering from migraine headaches.

Many books on the subject of creativity have been published for use by business executives and various students of the arts. But my heart beats for laborers in the Lord's harvest field. We are not competitors in a public-relations contest or even denominational strategists; we are followers of Christ who need to use this simple explanation to do our jobs better.

This book is not a compendium of clever and catchy ideas but a word of encouragement, a bit of know-how to enrich your heavenly calling. I can't make you become more creative, but I can place a tool in your hands if you are an eager and teachable disciple. Like a potter's wheel, your mind needs to receive the moist clay of ideas that require turning and shaping for new and beautiful ways of presenting the critical message of eternal life in Christ.

Walt Disney, arguably among the most creative individuals America has ever produced, was drawing flowers in his elementary-school class-room. His teacher looked at his paper and remonstrated, "Walter, flowers do not have faces!" He answered, "Mine do!"

I want to help you put faces on your flowers—to color outside your lines.

Acknowledgments

None of us is as smart as all of us.

—STEVE JOBS

Have you ever had an itch on your back that you can't reach? This book has been a burr under my mental saddle for a long time, begging to be written and daring me to tackle the tide of distrust about creative effort that lurks around our Christian enclaves. Only with a host of able craftsmen has it reached this working model.

To the myriad of authors and experts who have thought and written before me, I owe a profound debt of gratitude. Many of their works and resources are listed in the back of this book. For a legislature of professors and supervisors over the years who have critiqued and coached me, sometimes without mercy, I am most grateful. A particular word of thanks goes to Doug Smart of Roswell, Georgia, for passing along to us a magnificent list of "paradigm shifters," among other material.

But the crew of hardworking hands who have hoisted the sails on this vessel are especially noteworthy. My son, Bill, deserves high praise for his ingenious perseverance with my clumsy, cliché-ridden copy. Jim Howard, like a zealous squirrel caching nuts for the winter, has masterfully organized the voluminous resource material. My wife, Jeanne, has coaxed words into sentences and danced with paragraphs, all the while risking her sanity in a steep learning curve on a new computer. My administrative assistant, Pam Cole, has patiently pulled me off the wall time and again. And Roy Zuck has provided timely, attentive, and seasoned management to the process of delivering a publishable manuscript.

One thing I have learned (again): Creative desire and potential may show up as a loner, but creative products, results, outgrowth, or any masterpiece is borne of teamwork. Many people sense that something new needs to be done in ministry, but only a few step up and volunteer. *Together* we make things happen. Never underestimate the power of your neighbor!

Creativity—
Who Needs It?

*In a time of great change we are most
in need of creativity and innovation.*

—JOHN NAISBITT

In 1899, Charles Duell, Commissioner of the United States Office of
Patents, recommended shutting down the agency. "Everything that can
be invented has been invented," he declared.

Some today would recommend similar shuttering of the church.
The church, in their view, has become anachronistic, the vestige of a
bygone era, the last gasp of an authoritarian age, a creaking institution that has done what good it is capable of doing and now ought to
give way to more effective and relevant agencies.

Has the church outrun its usefulness?

- In 1900 the overwhelming majority of missionaries came from the West
  and traveled to remote areas to translate the Scriptures into primitive
  languages for unreached peoples. Today the West *hosts* as many missionaries as it sends, and students from every region of the developing
  world come to western universities where they encounter the gospel in
  English.

- In 1900 there was one primary source for the teaching of Christian
  beliefs: the local pulpit of the neighborhood church. Today countless
  forms of Christian expression exist among a mind-numbing variety

1

of churches, parachurch ministries, magazines, newsletters, radio programs, videotapes, CDs, Internet sites, and on and on.

- In 1900 the most stable form of the local church was a congregation of about two hundred people led by one pastor. Today the term *local church* defies definition. Megachurches with thousands of attendees are led by entire teams of pastors and staff. And online congregations are forming that may eliminate geographic considerations altogether.

Has the church outlived its usefulness?

If you think it has, consider the wisdom of G. K. Chesterton, noted Christian essayist of a bygone era. Saucy as always, he noted that at least five times in history "the faith has to all appearances gone to the dogs. In each of these five cases, it was the dog that died."[1]

So much for the church's demise. As with the patent office, I believe the church's best days are yet ahead. And yet, it's fair to ask, Has *your* church outlived its usefulness? Will it still have something to contribute even five years from now?

Only if it embraces change. For change is the ocean in which our society swims. As Charles Handy of the London School of Economics has put it, we inhabit an age of discontinuity, a chaotic time in which the rate of change itself is accelerating rapidly.

Is it possible for your church to survive, let alone thrive, amid such chaos? Absolutely! But it will require more than "business as usual." Above all, it will require *creativity*—the ability to envision and embrace a new future.

Please understand, the unshakeable foundation of our faith is Jesus Christ and His unchanging Word. That is nonnegotiable. But this unchanging gospel itself produces change. Profound change! Change that transforms lives, communities, and whole societies.

Yet how many churches have adopted the motto "Come weal or come woe, our status is quo"? And how many followers of Christ today have become mired in the mediocrity of sameness? John Henry Newman warned, "Fear not that your life will come to an end, but that it will never have a beginning." Yet the life and work of too many Christians—including many in positions of leadership—is best expressed in the epitaph "Died, age 24. Buried, age 70." Their tombstones will read, "I came. I saw. I *concurred.*"

May that not be true of you! Instead, I invite you to a life of new beginnings. That's what this book is about—the *newness* of life in Christ, the creative, redemptive side of our salvation. Every creative act is a re-affirmation that we serve the *Creator* God. Indeed, in an age of chaotic change the ability to embrace the new may well be one of the greatest apologetics we have as believers.

To that end, my aim is to produce churches and church leaders that are

- fully alive,
- growing,
- changing and becoming a change element,
- resourceful,
- flexible, and
- maladjusted to the status quo.

So let's begin with two compelling questions: What do we know for sure about creativity? And what will creativity do for you?

What Do We Know for Sure about Creativity?

There are many misconceptions about creative thinking. In this book I hope to clear away some of the myths with straightforward information. Here are five important facts to consider.

First, there is no one without significant creative potential. Nothing has been more convincingly proven, both by research and in the laboratory of life. I have taught principles of creativity to children, teenagers, adults, and senior citizens; to the gifted and the retarded; to professionals and blue-collar workers; to men and women; to people in both the Western world and developing nations, including more than seventy-five overseas locations.

In all that experience I have never found an exception to the principle that *every* person has at least some ability to be creative. And of course, that includes *you.* You are a creative individual, whether you have ever thought of yourself that way, and whether you seem to be functioning that way. You are a creative individual! At least potentially.

"But I've been told I'm *not* creative," you may be saying. Don't believe a word of it! Tony Buzan hit the nail with his head when he reasoned, "You who still doubt your own abilities have yourself learned to talk and to read. You should, therefore, find it difficult to attack a position of which you yourself are evidence for the defense."[2]

"The concept is interesting and well-formed, but in order to earn better than a 'C', the idea must be feasible."

—Yale University management professor commenting on Fred Smith's paper proposing a reliable overnight delivery system. Smith eventually founded Federal Express Corporation, known today as FedEx.

May I submit that if you deny your creativity, you suggest a deficiency in God's creation. The idea that only a gifted minority of human beings are creative is one of the most persistent and pernicious myths there is. It is totally false. Yet it dies with great difficulty.

To be sure, creativity must be developed, then disciplined, before it can finally be deployed. But what we must never doubt is that it exists in each one of us. Part of our difficulty in accepting this truth is that even though each of us is born to live creatively, we have different creative gifts to work with.

Moreover, there's a vast difference between comprehension and practice. Reading a book about swimming is one thing; diving into a pool is quite another. You may learn about swimming by reading, but you learn to swim by swimming. Likewise, you learn to be creative by practicing the principles of creativity.

One other reason why many of us doubt our creative capacities is the large gap that may exist between our creative potential and our creative productivity. Having never turned out a masterpiece, we are prone to conclude, "I'm not very creative."

But we need to develop the mentality of Michelangelo, who, upon viewing a piece of marble on one occasion, is reported to have said, "There is an angel imprisoned in it, and I must set it free!" Don't deny your creative giftedness; release it!

"God surrounds himself with incompetents. The people God uses have rarely been great people, nor have great people been the people God uses. God looks for misfits and milquetoasts, shmucks and schlemiels. It's not that he has to make-do with a bunch of fools. He *chooses* them."

—*David Roper*

That is what I aim to accomplish in this book. You may be blind to your own, God-given capacities, not unlike the blind man from Bethsaida who was brought before Jesus. After spitting in his eyes and touching them with His hands, the Lord asked him, "Do you see anything?" At first he replied, "I see people; they look like trees walking around." Only when the Savior opened his eyes fully did the man see everything clearly (Mark 8:22–26). My prayer is that the same will be true for you when it comes to recognizing your innate creativity!

This brings us to a second fact that helps explain our difficulty in accepting the first one.

Second, conditioning is often fatal to the creative process. One of the main reasons so many people seem to lack creativity is that the creative sparks they actually do possess have been doused by years of negative conditioning. We'll examine the causes for this later, but the fact is universal.

Here's an exercise to illustrate what I mean. The picture below shows a side view of a proposed design for a wheelbarrow.

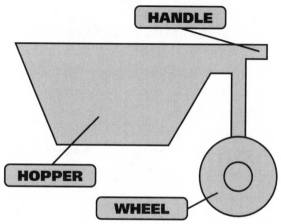

Write down five comments about this design.

Now go back and examine your comments carefully. Do you see a general theme? Are they all, or most of them, critical? If you are like most people, your comments may look something like this:

1. The wheel is too small.
2. The handle is too short.
3. It's poorly balanced.
4. It won't hold much.
5. (Some version of . . .) It's stupid . . . ridiculous . . . ha-ha-ha!

Do these echo your comments? If so, may I point out that you were asked to comment on the design, not crucify it!

Why do so many of us feel a compulsion to criticize, to focus on flaws, to denigrate a new idea?

> **"Professor Goddard does not know the relation between action and reaction and the need to have something better than a vacuum against which to react. He seems to lack the basic knowledge ladled out daily in high schools."**
>
> —1921 New York Times *editorial criticizing Robert Goddard, father of modern rocketry*

If you've received higher education, you are probably even more critical than most. Why? Because you were trained to be! You were schooled in the art of *critical* thinking. That's not all bad, but it can be limiting.

When children are shown the design above, they often become keenly excited. They have not yet acquired the adult propensity for constant fault-finding. Here are some typical observations children make.

"It's a very interesting wheelbarrow. Because the handle is so short, if you get some mud on the wheel, you can reach over and kick it off."

"Hey, that's a neat wheelbarrow! Why, you could wheel it right up to the edge of a hole and empty it."

"Yeah, and that design gives you the opportunity to put a little trap door in the bottom of the hopper and empty it easily just by pulling the string."

Let's go to school on these comments; they prove highly instructive.

For one thing, they bear out a principle I have found useful: Whenever confronted with a new idea, always ask at least three questions.

What's positive about this idea? Your perspective always determines your product. *What's interesting about it?* Initially, don't feel obligated to support or criticize the idea. Curious comments are far more creative than critical ones. *What can we change to improve the idea* (particularly if there's a negative reaction)?

Third, negative conditioning can be reversed. It seems inevitable that many people will be conditioned not to be creative. Yet, it is possible to peel off the layers of negativity, though not without effort and cost. The reeducation process comes with a high price tag and is not available from a cut-rate pushcart vendor.

Actually, it is creative people themselves who pay the price the non-creative among us are unwilling to pay—a brutal fact we try to avoid. Breaking the mold can be hard, persistent work, even for the pros. However, there's a payoff to that persistence.

Fourth, creativity is a lifestyle of adventure. This is key. To be most effective, creativity must pervade all of life—from writing letters to wrapping Christmas presents, from preparing meals to making love. It does not exist in isolation. It is not suddenly turned on. One can never sit down and say, "I shall now proceed to be creative." Creativity affects one's thinking, behavior, attitudes, values, and communication.

"Any life that has vitality carries an element of adventure," wrote Bob Buford. "To give up adventure is to give up a great deal of what not only makes life interesting, but what gives it a certain destiny or purpose. The risk of the unfamiliar can be unsettling, but it is often balanced with the security in knowing that you are en route to doing and being what God designed for you."[3]

Perhaps on reading these words, you are tempted to fall back into the old mind-set that says, "Well, I'm just not the creative type. Never have been, never will be." And you throw your hands up in despair. If so, be assured by a fifth fact.

Fifth, creativity can be learned. We are not talking about something mystical or magic. This is not a case of "some have it, and some don't." Creativity is like honey in one's mental beehive: It's food for the esthetic part of living, but it's also a practical alternative to the sterility of merely subsisting on nuts and bolts.

Christian educator Marlene LeFever says that creativity is the ability to see things in a new way. She cites Graham Wallas, who, in 1927, suggested a simple five-step process to get one's creative juices flowing: (1) preparation (flirting with anything new); (2) incubation (mixing with other ideas to yield new combinations); (3) illumination (new, sometimes off-the-wall ideas); (4) elaboration (building and refining); and (5) verification (confirming that the end product is worthwhile).[4]

This book is designed toward that end—first to convince you that creativity is not a luxury but a necessity, and then to equip you to unleash your own creative capacity.

What Will Creativity Do for You?

What are the gains if you buy into this message and practice these methods? How will creativity affect your life and ministry? Let me suggest five benefits yielded by living creatively.

Creativity will perpetuate the learning process. As long as you live, you learn; as long as you learn, you live. If you stop learning today you stop living tomorrow. Therefore our task is to develop lifelong learners.

Most readers of this book have probably taken courses leading to a degree—but not necessarily to an education. For most people, education is the process of passing from unconscious to conscious ignorance. It's whatever is left over after you've forgotten the facts.

But real education is a process, not an instant package. "The person who has ceased to learn ought not be allowed to wander around loose in these dangerous days," someone once said. That's a perceptive comment. For when one has ceased to learn, he not only shrivels, but he also tends to stifle everyone else nearby.

"Not to be fortified with good ideas is to be victimized by bad ones."

—Carl F. H. Henry

Peter urged us to "grow in grace and in knowledge of our Lord and Savior Jesus Christ" (2 Pet. 3:18). The Greek verb for *grow* conveys the sense that we are to *continue* to grow in that grace and knowledge. Spiritual maturation is an *ongoing process.*

Notice the order and the balance: first grace, followed by knowledge. Some Christians are very gracious. They are like Saint Bernard dogs, slobbering all over you. If only they had a modicum of biblical knowledge! Meanwhile, others excel in knowledge. Why, they practically know more than the apostle Paul! Do you doubt it? Just ask them. You could wish they had one scintilla of graciousness! Christians like that could stand to learn Hebrews 5:8, which informs us that "although he [Jesus] was a son, he learned obedience." How? Through "what he suffered." Suffering is God's melting pot to shape the soul. And none of us is exempt from the process. God's curriculum is not an elective; it is a required course designed to make us like His Son, Jesus Christ.

Five Ways to "Stay Ahead of the Curve"

1. Learn to be a better listener.
2. Once a week, read a trade magazine from a different industry.
3. Let your kids tutor you in a subject they know more about than you do.
4. Volunteer.
5. Read what has stood the test of time.

—Watts Wacker, resident futurist at SRI International

As we continue to learn, we discover a second benefit of creativity.

Creativity helps us meet the growing demands of a changing society and church. We used to be told there were only two things we could be sure of—death and taxes. But now we can add a third: *change!*

Our culture is experiencing exponential growth in the quantity and/or complexity of virtually every area of society—especially human knowledge. At its 1994 convention the World Future Society estimated that human knowledge will *double* every seventy-three days by the year 2020. In turn, whole new systems of learning and communication will be required for people to cope with these accelerating developments and the changes they bring.

But change is not just a cultural fact; it's a biblical fact too. Romans 8:28 teaches that we are "predestined to be conformed to the image of Christ." Imagine that—becoming *like Christ*. If that is true, how much change do you think you can expect?

Yet the question nags: Are those of us who are church leaders preparing our people for change? I'm not so sure. In fact, I sometimes wonder whether the evangelical church will catch up with the twentieth century before it enters the twenty-first.

It is always a delicate assignment to distinguish what is cultural from what is biblical. Biblical truth is fixed and nonnegotiable. It cannot change. But the cultural climate varies constantly and must always be negotiated. The former focuses on revelation, the latter on relevance. Thus as society changes rapidly, significantly, and pervasively, our methods must also change, even though the gospel message never changes. But I wonder whether we know the difference.

One pastor expressed it vividly: "Hendricks, I find it easier to change the doctrinal statement of my congregation than to change the flowers in the sanctuary." He added that their favorite hymn was "We Shall Not Be Moved."

Many of us are inveterate preservers of our traditionalism!

Some time ago I was invited to evaluate the program of a local church. Frankly, this church had the finest program I had ever seen—for 1946! They had been on hold for decades. I learned they had a financial problem, and while evaluating this with their leaders I suggested a solution for their problem. "Why don't you build a fence around this church and charge admission for people to come in and see what it was like in the previous generation?" After that, we had a meaningful discussion, lasting well past midnight. As a result of some significant changes, that church is now growing again.

Living in this generation requires adaptability. We need to hear the Lord's words to Jeremiah: "If you have raced with men on foot and they have worn you out, how can you compete with horses? If you stumble in safe country, how will you manage in the thickets by the Jordan?" (Jer. 12:5).

Trust me, the days to come will find us in a footrace with more than just horses, and in thickets more treacherous than the Jordan's. What we face will test more than our courage; it will test our creativity. In the words of the eminent historian Arnold Toynbee, "To give a fair chance to potential creativity is a matter of life or death for any society."

Perhaps our greatest challenge will be in how we present our message, which brings us to a third value of creativity.

Creativity will infect our communication with freshness and vitality. Stanley Marcus, of Neiman Marcus Department Store fame, wrote, "When I look at the same old things, I think the same old thoughts, but when the furniture is changed, my thinking changes. . . . Routine is the enemy of creative thinking."[5]

Even though Marcus had merchandizing in mind, his point still applies to those of us with a heavenly mission in mind. We need to pursue what Eric Hoffer calls "the passionate state of mind," not imitating shopworn methods of sharing the good news. The accompanying chart shows an intriguing study of the relationship between one's predictability and one's impact in communication. Note that the study involves methodology, not morals.

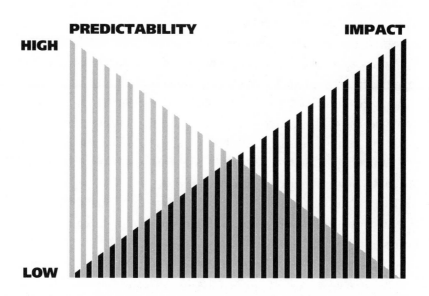

Nowhere is the unanticipated—a hallmark of creativity—more obvious than in the life and ministry of our Lord. On one occasion the Pharisees and Herodians, usually enemies of each other, were welded in opposition against the Savior and His teaching. The issue? Paying taxes—always a controversial matter.

"Is it permissible for Jews to pay taxes to Caesar?" they asked Him. They thought they had Him trapped. Whether He said yes or no, they were convinced they would win; at least, one of the opposing groups would win.

But Jesus asked, "Do you have a coin?" "Certainly." "Whose inscription is on it?" "Caesar's," they replied.

Then what's your problem? "Give to Caesar what is Caesar's, and to God what is God's" (Matt. 22:21).

Every Jew learned from his earliest age that stamped on him was the image of God. So Jesus was using their own teaching against them: Give to Caesar what is rightfully his (taxes/money), and give to God what is rightfully His (life/dedication).

Can't you just see them, those Pharisaical faces with puzzled looks, leading to the quiet query, "Who thought up this dumb question?"

Whenever anybody thought he had Jesus figured out, the Lord slipped up on his blind side. Never did the Savior approach any two evangelistic or educational situations in quite the same way. Creativity was His hallmark.

And so it should be ours. That's one reason why modeling is so critical in ministry. Are we a model to others in our church community, particularly its young people? Are they irresistibly drawn to the service of our Lord because of the excitement and dynamic that characterizes our efforts? Or are they repelled from becoming involved because they have been watching us and are convinced there must be a better way to invest one's life? How attractive and inviting are we?

This is a crucial question, because the crying need of the church today is leadership. Creativity plays a major role in meeting that need, which brings us to another observation about creativity.

Creativity will develop our leadership potential. There is a strong correlation between creativity and leadership effectiveness. Leaders are visionaries, not people in a rut. They tend to see further, probe more deeply, and think more insightfully than others. How do they cultivate these qualities? By constantly dipping into new ideas, experiences, and relationships that keep them fresh and on their toes.

For example, Peter Drucker, expert on modern management from the Claremont Graduate School, has been called by *Forbes Magazine* the most perceptive observer of the American scene since Alexis de Tocqueville. "Still the Youngest Mind" was the name of the cover story featuring this renowned eighty-eight-year-old thinker. How does he stay so current, yet so profound?

One reason is that every three years he undertakes the study of some subject he has never before investigated. He reads indepth on that topic. He travels to places associated with it. He corresponds with experts. And he compares what he learns with prior ideas and knowledge.

This is a highly creative endeavor! And the results speak for themselves. But I find it particularly interesting because a lot of people tend to think that a man of Drucker's years and wisdom hardly needs to be bothered with what he *doesn't* know. Yet the essence of the creative leader is that he embraces the new and the unexplored as an opportunity.

By the way, when was the last time *you* picked up a book on a topic that had nothing whatever to do with your area of expertise?

Creativity can overhaul our lives. Jesus said, "I have come that they may have life, and have it to the full" (John 10:10). "To the full"? Yes! In effect, "I mean *really* live!" Are you living or just existing? Are you excited by the truth or embalmed by it? Is the Christian life a drag or a delight?

Eternal life is much more than quantity of life—it's a quality of living. Jesus' prayer in John 17 lists seven characteristics of eternal life, but six are *present* possessions; only one is eternal (an eternal home in heaven). So eternal life begins here and now.

That's why our Lord invited the multitude, "Come to me, all you who are weary and burdened, and I will give you. . . ." Give you what? Burnout? No! "Rest!" How? Because "my yoke is easy, and my burden is light" (Matt. 11:28, 30). This suggests that if your Christian life has become painful, you are carrying a yoke or burden that belongs to someone else. It certainly is not the yoke of the Lord.

Yet we have so many weary ones in the faith today. In fact, a layman once asked me one of those thought-provoking questions that dust your mind with itching powder, "Hendricks, how many men and women over fifty-five do you know who are still tracking for Jesus Christ?" Intellectual honesty compelled me to reply, "Not that many."

That's a tragedy! Yet the prevailing direction for many senior saints is toward retirement and a rocking chair. Why? Too often it's because they have given up; there is no more creative spark left.

By the way, if I'm describing you, then let me further challenge your mind with this thought: You may retire from a career; indeed, you may have no other option. But you *never* retire from the service of the King. So what are you doing *today* to accomplish His purposes?

Too many believers die with an unsung song still in them. They finish life at the top of the pile in their field but at the bottom of life in terms of fulfillment. Having lost their purpose, they rapidly lose their life. The meaning is missing, because creativity has cratered.

Say Good-bye to the Ordinary Life

Why be creative? Why me? Why you? Because the Incarnation banished ordinariness. Dorothy Sayers put it graphically.

> The people who hanged Christ never . . . accused Him of being a bore— on the contrary; they thought Him too dynamic to be safe. It has been left for later generations to muffle up that shattering personality and surround Him with an atmosphere of tedium. We have efficiently pared the claws of the Lion of Judah, certified Him "meek and mild," and recommended Him as a fitting household pet for pale curates and pious old ladies. To those who knew Him, however, He in no way suggested a milk-and-water person; *they* objected to Him as a dangerous firebrand. True, He was tender to the unfortunate, patient with honest inquirers, and humble before Heaven, but He insulted respectable clergymen by calling them hypocrites; He referred to King Herod as "that fox"; He went to parties in disreputable company and was looked upon as a "gluttonous man and a wine bibber, a friend of publicans and sinners"; He assaulted indignant tradesmen and threw them and their belongings out of the Temple; He drove a coach-and-horses through a number of sacrosanct and hoary regulations; He cured diseases by any means

that came handy, with a shocking casualness in the matter of other people's pigs and property. . . . He was emphatically not a dull man in His human lifetime, and if He was God, there can be nothing dull about God either.[6]

If Christ is dull, one may ask, what is worthy to be called exciting? His beauty makes us ugly; His sensitivity makes us calloused; His uniqueness makes us wearisome.

Exercises

1. How would you evaluate your own creative potential? Generally speaking, do you see yourself as a creative or uncreative individual? Why?

2. Use the following inventory to assess your creativity:

	True	False
A. Once I have made up my mind, I seldom change it.	___	___
B. I am very careful about my manner of dress.	___	___
C. I am often so annoyed when someone tries to get ahead of me in a line of people that I speak to him about it.	___	___
D. I always follow the rule "Business before pleasure."	___	___
E. Compared to my own self-respect, the respect of others means very little.	___	___
F. At times I have been so entertained by the cleverness of a crook that I have hoped he would get away with it.	___	___
G. I don't like to work on a problem unless there is a possibility of coming out with a clear-cut and unambiguous answer.	___	___

H. I commonly wonder what hidden reason
another person may have for doing
something nice for me. ___ ___

I. Sometimes I rather enjoy going against
the rules and doing things I'm not
supposed to do. ___ ___

J. I like to fool around with new ideas
even if they turn out later to be a total
waste of time. ___ ___

K. I get annoyed with writers who go out
of their way to use strange and unusual
words. ___ ___

L. For most questions there is just one
right answer, once a person is able to
get all the facts. ___ ___

M. I would like the job of a foreign
correspondent for a newspaper. ___ ___

N. Every teen ought to get away from
his family for a year or two while
he is still in his teens. ___ ___

O. The trouble with many people is
that they don't take things
seriously enough. ___ ___

3. Generate a list of ways in which you have displayed creativity in the past week or month. Think carefully!

4. Review your responses to the wheelbarrow design exercise in this chapter. In what ways were your responses different from those of the children? In what ways were they similar?

5. How would you like to benefit by increasing your creativity?

6. Name five people whom you think of as highly creative, and why. Ask a friend to do the same. Then compare your lists and discuss the question, What makes a person creative?

Helpful Resource

- Wilson, Craig McNair. *Recapturing Your Creative Spirit.* Videotape, available from Dynamic Communications International, P.O. Box 745940, Arvada, CO, 80006-5940. Tel: 303-425-1319; e-mail: dcw@kendavis.com; website: www.kendavis.com.

Creativity— What Is It?

Eternal truths will be neither true nor eternal unless they have fresh meaning for every new social situation.

—FRANKLIN D. ROOSEVELT

2

Charles Kettering observed that a problem well defined is a problem half solved. So what exactly are we talking about when we use the slippery term *creativity?* In this chapter we will explore what creativity is not and then what it is. In the process we will discover that creativity is a phenomenon more often experienced than an abstraction to be defined.

What Creativity Is Not

We turn first to the negative. As we saw in the last chapter, there are many myths about creativity. Many of them stem from false assumptions of what creativity is.

Creativity is not change for the sake of change. The creative process and product invariably involves change, but not all change is creative. A debilitating disease may involve major life change, but it is not creative change.

Creativity is not always beneficial. Human beings have learned to split the atom—a revolutionary change! The possibilities for good from this new technology are staggering. Yet so are the possibilities for dire consequences and the destructive use of nuclear fission.

In the spiritual realm the apostle Paul suffered a "thorn in the flesh." Paul earnestly prayed for God to remove this thorn, but he was refused. And yet the apostle's ministry became refreshingly creative as God's incredible grace was supplied in his place of need (2 Cor. 12:9).

Creativity is not an end in itself. Creativity is a means to achieving something better, something more salutary, productive, or beautiful. It exists for improvement, not impression. It never freezes progress; it forwards it. The gift is given for a purpose: The chief end of man is to glorify God, not man.

Creativity is not always original. C. S. Lewis furnishes a crucial caveat: "'Creation' as applied to human authorship seems to me to be an entirely misleading term. We rearrange elements [God] has provided. There is not a vestige of real creativity *de novo* in us. Try to imagine a new primary color, a third sex, a further dimension, or even a monster which does not consist of bits of existing animals stuck together. Nothing happens. And that surely is why our works . . . never mean to others quite what we intended: because we are re-combining elements made by Him and already containing *His* meanings."[1]

Sometimes creativity is merely the discovery of ideas and behavior already employed in another generation or location but not noticed or applied in the here and now. That's why the study of history is so important and can be highly stimulating to the creative process. Not that we live in the past, but we need to learn from it. The past is a springboard, not a sofa. Historical amnesia is costly, for it dooms us to repeat the errors of a previous age.

George Marsden, professor of history at the University of Notre Dame, notes, "If history has any lesson for us . . . it is that the church is often most healthy when it is at odds with the culture's standards. That does not mean we have to renounce the evangelical successes . . . but it suggests that we should view them as an occasion for chastening self-examination as much as for celebration."[2]

Learning from history is a process of filtering, holding on to what is beneficial and worth repeating, but discarding what is harmful and destructive.

Creativity is not the exclusive property of a few creative geniuses. Many people needlessly demean their own imaginative powers. Discouragement clouds their understanding. Yet creativity is a seed waiting to sprout up in each one of us. If creativity seems to be lacking, it is rarely due to a deficit in brain power, but rather to feelings that are skewed and distorted. The root problem is a lost sense of wonder.

On the other hand, ponder an overriding positive aspect of creativity: It is lastingly constructive. Ironically, what often passes for creativity can only be called destructive. Eugene Peterson makes a thoughtful assertion in this regard: "Violent action is the antithesis of creative action. When we no longer have the will or the patience to be creative, we attempt to express our will by coercion."[3]

Many of us resemble the proverbial blind men describing the elephant. Our comprehension is limited to the particular part of the elephantine anatomy within our restricted sphere. To refine our meager understanding, we would benefit from the insight of professionals who have lived with this elusive term and managed to package its quicksilver-like meaning with precision and accuracy.

What Creativity Is

As there is no single, unifying definition of creativity, I want to switch on the current in your thinking and stimulate your mind to produce your own definition.

I should point out that some masters of this subject focus on the creative *person*, others on the creative *process*, and others on the creative *product*:

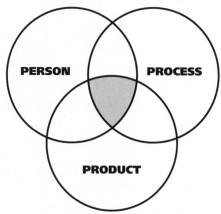

Person/Process/Product[4]

The verb *create* derives from a Latin word meaning "to grow." According to *Webster's Dictionary,* the term carries the sense of bringing into existence, investing with a new form, bringing about by a course of action or behavior, causing through imaginative skill, or designing something new.

Funk and Wagnalls Dictionary ties creativity to production: to originate, be the cause of, produce from thought and imagination, be the first to portray, as a character or part.

Note that the terms *creative, innovative, inventive, imaginative,* and *original* are often used interchangeably in dictionary definitions.

How do experts define this term? Here is a brief sampling:

- Betty Edwards, professor of art, California State University, Long Beach: "A creative person is one who can process in new ways the information directly at hand, the ordinary sensory data available to all of us."

- Rudolf Fleseh, bestselling author of *The Art of Clear Thinking* and *The Art of Clear Writing:* "Creative thinking may mean simply the realization that there is no particular virtue in doing things the way they always have been done."

- Robert W. Olson, researcher: "The secret to creativity lies in making the familiar strange. Ultimately all creativity springs from curiosity."

- Albert Szent Gyorgyi, Nobel Prize-winning physician: "Discovery consists of looking at the same things as everyone else and thinking something different."

- E. Paul Torrance, professor and researcher: "The process of becoming sensitive to or aware of problems, deficiencies, gaps in knowledge, missing elements, disharmonies, and so on. Bringing together in new relationships available existing information, defining the difficulty of identifying the missing elements; searching for solutions, making guesses, or formulating hypotheses about the problems or deficiencies; testing and retesting these hypotheses and modifying and retesting them; perfecting them; and finally, communicating the results."

- Sydney J. Parnes et al., of the Creative Education Foundation: "The essence of the concept of creativity might be considered to be the association of thoughts, facts, and ideas, etc., into a new and relevant configuration, one that has meaning beyond the sum of the parts—that provides a synergistic effect. The product . . . may be new and relevant to a group or organization, to society as a whole, or merely to the individual concerned."

The bottom line? *Creativity is the generation of unique, innovative thoughts, actions, and feelings, with appropriate implementation for the benefit of others. It often means little more than the ability of perceiving in an unhabitual way. It is a function of knowledge, imagination, and evaluation.*

Stripped, then, to its barest essentials, creativity consists of three essential characteristics:

1. *Novelty.* Both in associations and arrangements, creativity involves something that has not been thought, seen, developed, used, or implemented before. Words like *new, strange, innovative,* and *different* would describe it.

2. *Usefulness.* Creativity has functional value. It does something positive for people or the environment in a utilitarian manner. Key terms here would include *effective, helping, solving a problem, enchanting, educational, persuasive, entertaining,* or *stimulating.* There is always improvement—always better, but never the best. Change occurs not for the sake of change but for a useful purpose.

3. *Reproducibility.* Creative outcomes raise the hope that in the future, other results like them can be produced. They are transferable, in terms of both process and product. They do not involve random events that are unrepeatable and unpredictable.

Taken together, these three qualities suggest that creativity is novelty that is useful and reproducible.

What Does Creativity Mean for You?

In the end, what matters is not so much the meaning of creativity as an abstraction but its meaning as an expression of you. What does it mean for you to be the creative individual God made you to be?

In every case true creativity is a change of direction. Remember, however, that not all change is good. Some things must never change. For example:

- The Lord never changes (Mal. 3:6).

- The Word of God never changes (Isa. 40:8).

- Human nature (the "heart," to use a biblical term) never changes (Rom. 3:23).

- The moral law of God (for example, the Ten Commandments) never changes (Exod. 20:2–17).

I will never forget the renowned artisan I was privileged to meet in Australia. This craftsman creates exquisite sculptures of birds out of pure silver. He related in my hearing something of his creative process. First, he makes a detailed study of the bird he intends to portray. He learns about its flight patterns, its habitat, its mating rituals, and its nest. He becomes something of an expert on these beautiful creatures.

But there is more to his preparation. For years he apprenticed himself to an older craftsman to learn the secrets of metallurgy and sculpture. Through this man he learned about the properties of silver, the use of the tools, and the economics of the art.

All of this was merely getting ready for the effort. Only after careful thought and study and intense concentration was he ready to define what it was he wanted to do creatively. Only then was he able to realize his dream.

So it is for each of us. The formulation of our own creative dreams demands that we grasp the ropes of our grounded balloons, so to speak, by identifying our unique strengths, convictions, and aspirations. Finally convinced that they are airworthy, we can then release them to soar.

G. K. Chesterton said, "A saint is one who exaggerates what the world neglects." What are you prepared to exaggerate, to the glory of God?

Exercises

1. Devise an original definition of *creativity* with which you are comfortable. It might help to use an object, an analogy, a visual, or a drama.
2. Look up the definition of *creativity* in a dictionary. Why is a good definition important for any subject?
3. Discover as many definitions as possible for *creativity*. Consult books, articles, newspapers, word finders, speeches, and so on.
4. Evaluate the following definition of *creativity:* "The creation of the new, or the rearranging of the old in new ways."
5. Theodore Levitt of the Harvard Business School coined the phrase "creative imitation." Does that sound like a contradiction in terms? Is it possible to be "creative" (which has the idea of originality) yet "imitative" (which does not)?
6. Recall the three essential characteristics of creativity: novelty, usefulness, and reproducibility. How might "creative imitation" fit these criteria?

Creativity–
Is It Biblical?

'Tis wise to learn; 'tis godlike to create.

—JOHN GODFREY SAXE

3

We humans are quite convinced that all original ideas are man-made. We never outgrow our toddler talk, "Look, Mommy, what I did!" As Christians we recognize our bent toward pride and we repudiate it, vowing to be humble, pious, principled, and above all, biblical.

Perhaps for that reason, creative and original ideas smack of carnality to many of us. So we need to consider the question, Does creativity have scriptural sanction? Or is it just another modern gimmick, soon to be condemned to the ash heap of history like hundreds of other trendy ideas? Is it optional or essential to Christian truth and life?

Creative Christians root their study of creativity in the rich, fertile soil of the Bible. There, God has inviting, exciting, and creatively wrapped packages that beg to be opened. A procedure of discovery awaits an eager, creative Bible student.

Similarly, our divinely designed ecosystem has no garbage. Nothing is a throwaway. It seems that God has structured life as a kind of treasure hunt. All we have to do is unwrap the packages; there is a profound, and yet playful, surprise aspect to creative living that eludes many adults.

Elizabeth Barrett Browning caught something of this mystery with her lines:

> Earth's crammed with heaven,
> And every common bush afire with God;
> But only he sees who takes off his shoes,
> The rest sit round it and pluck blackberries.

As an educator, I believe the process is as important as the product. Therefore you should use this chapter as a stimulus, not a substitute, for personal Bible study. Build your own case for creativity from the Scriptures. The thoughts presented here are designed to provoke, not to paralyze, your own thinking in this critical area. Our approach is selective, not exhaustive.

Creativity is demanded by at least four indicators: the nature of our God, the nature of humans, the nature of our salvation, and the nature of our calling. Let's take these in turn.

The Nature of Our God

"What comes into our minds when we think about God," said A. W. Tozer, "is the most important thing about us."[1] This central concept of ultimate authority controls the eternal welfare of every individual. Of all the questions a rational person must address in life, undoubtedly the most vital one concerns the nature of our God.

Our task as Christians is to be informed accurately about the truth we believe. The venerable theologian Carl F. H. Henry reminds us that "despite the knowledge explosion of our times, few people of today—church-goers included—seem to know what God wills, what Scripture says, and what Jesus taught."[2] The revolutionary message of the gospel, when clarified by the Holy Spirit, gives us new eyes to see Him.

God's first attention-getter is His natural world. He created it before human beings were made. It is the first thing any of us sees. But do we understand it as an expression of who God is?

One of the richest descriptions of God's creative handiwork sparkles

28

in the gemstones of the saga of Job. Here is a good man, successful in every human endeavor and without blame before his Creator. Inexplicably (from the human point of view), he loses it all in a series of disasters. Then, sitting on an ash heap, surrounded by his friends-turned-analysts, he hears the voice of his Maker asking, "Who is this that darkens my counsel with words without knowledge?" (Job 38:1).

Then the Creator proceeds with a mother lode of information, framed in a series of rhetorical questions (38:3–40:3). This exam opens a window on creation from God's viewpoint, providing His take on His handiwork: "Where were you . . . ?" "Do you know . . . ?" "Can you . . . ?" "Can anyone . . . ?"

The only replies Job can muster are, "I am unworthy," "I put my hand over my mouth," and "I have no answer." (40:4–5). Thus the exuberance of God's creative handiwork overwhelms His human creature; but it also serves to provoke adoration and provides a template for humanity's own endeavors. Job—and we—learn to behold God through His handiwork and to learn from Him. We partner with Him to accomplish His purposes.

J. I. Packer observed, "There is nothing irrational about believing that God who made the world can still intrude creativity in it." The God revealed in Scripture loves diversity. No two snowflakes are completely identical. Each rose petal has an individual print. God did not stop with a thousand or so insects but conjured up 300,000 species of beetles and weevils alone. His stars are numberless; so far we estimate there are 100 billion galaxies. Hugh Ross figures that there are 100 billion trillion stars.

No wonder David the psalmist could exclaim, "When I consider your heavens, the work of your fingers, the moon and the stars, which you have set in place, what is man that you are mindful of him?" (Ps. 8:3–4).

And if the planet on which we live is so magnificently adorned, what must He have built into His sons and daughters who are its caretakers? Weigh the words of the triune Godhead: "Let us make man in our image, in our likeness, and let them rule" (Gen. 1:26). The enormity of that decision can be understood only dimly by our limited minds.

Isaac Newton remarked, "In the absence of any other proof, the thumb alone would convince me of God's existence." This one extraordinary feature of the human hand, with its proficient range of motion, mirrors an inventive brilliance of astounding proportions. Again David exclaimed, "I praise you because I am fearfully and wonderfully made; your works are wonderful" (Ps. 139:14).

Every single baby of the billions born since Adam has arrived with a unique voice print, individual fingerprints, and a DNA like no one else's. Psalm 139:16 informs us that a custom-designed life plan has been crafted for each one. Page through an anatomy text, research the functions of the fifteen billion neurons in each human brain, interview a heart surgeon or an ear-nose-throat specialist, watch a baby form in the womb of a young woman and witness the subsequent birth. No rational individual could fail to conclude that these are phenomena beyond the scope of human explanation.

Everything our God touches reflects His creativity. He is the Maker and Lord of all. "For this is what the Lord says—he who created the heavens, he is God; he who fashioned and made the earth, he founded it; he did not create it to be empty, But formed it to be inhabited—he says; 'I am the Lord, and there is no other'" (Isa. 45:18).

The Nature of Humans—God's Highest Creation

Many Christians fancy a scenario at the entrance to heaven in which Peter asks new arrivals for their credentials. Admittance is granted when they cite their resumés, which they assume to be on file somewhere in the celestial archives. Although we can quote Ephesians 2:8–9 about being saved by grace, many of us harbor a secret bias in favor of a works-based salvation. We want to insist that God is somehow obligated to assign residences in His eternal home to those who have done good deeds. We hang on doggedly to the idea of doing something for God to earn His favor.

Such delusions flow from overindulgence in the same unreason that trapped Eve—and Adam—in the Garden. Sure (we say), God may have *said* it, but surely He didn't *mean* it the way it sounds. No, it has to make sense to *us*. And that is where the derailment has occurred.

And yet, despite our condition, fallen humans retain the imprint of the Creator, as described by John Calvin. "The human mind, fallen as it is, and corrupted from its integrity, is yet invested and adorned by God with excellent talents. If we believe that the Spirit of God is the only fountain of truth, we should neither reject nor despise the truth, wherever it shall appear, unless we wish to insult the Spirit of God."[3]

A fragment of thought dropped into my mind by Madeleine L'Engle surfaces here: Man has a viewpoint, but God has the view. As Christians, we must strive to align our warped viewpoint with God's omniscience. If we conceive of God as greater than our minds can grasp, we will worship Him in awe and wonder. His words will impact us deeply, and evil will trouble us significantly. But, if we insist on our own measurements, we will marginalize and trivialize His revealed Word, including His view of sin. Hence the insightful title of J. B. Phillips's book, *Your God Is Too Small*.[4]

"Men go abroad to wonder at the height of mountains, at the huge waves of the sea, at the long courses of the rivers, at the vast compass of the ocean, at the circular motion of the stars, and then pass by themselves without wondering." So spoke Augustine as he observed our lack of wonder about ourselves. Wheaton College professor Leland Ryken observes, "The fact that humans are created in God's image provides a sanction for human creativity and a theological explanation for why people create."[5]

Our amazing brain with all its inscrutable intricacies seems able to comprehend everything in the world except how to glorify God. For that reason, the full potential of the individual—which is the ultimate mission of Christian education—remains a frontier task. Humans are not dead fossils but living, pulsating, and spectacular creatures. "Why are we wide-eyed when contemplating the possibility that life may exist somewhere else in the universe," Norman Cousins asks, "but we wear blinders when contemplating the possibilities of life on earth?"[6]

As Christians, we know the answer to the question of where life originated, but we do not always demonstrate to the world what life can become. Ryken points to our daily rationale for creativity: "Human creativity is rooted in divine creativity. Artists create because God created first. Genesis 1 is the starting point for thinking Christianly about artistic creativity.... [God] is introduced as a creative artist ... like a painter working on a canvas ... until the picture was complete. He then pronounced his creation 'very good' (Gen. 1:31)."[7]

The Lord started the creative process, then delegated the ongoing work of creation to His creatures. Thus people, like God, are creators. A characteristic common to God and humanity is the desire and ability to make things. The image of God affirms human creativity as something good since it is an imitation of what God does. Every creative act is an imitation of Him. Essential as is the basis of our human creative ability in the image of God, this fact does not stand alone.

Human beings are created in the image of God, the *imago dei*. Thus we are designed to be like Him. He possesses not only intellect, emotions, and will—the essential ingredients of personality—but also a creative component. So it is incredible that many believers claim to be related to the most creative Person there is, yet act so noncreatively. What a distortion of God's image!

Our need is not better brains but a better use of the brains God has given us. We have nothing to do with the fact of life but everything to do with its meaning. The apostle John's first epistle explores the theme of "like Father, like son." God is light, he tells us; therefore, walk in the light. God is love; therefore, walk in love. God is life; therefore, walk in life. By the same argument, if God is creative, and we are created in His image, then we should prove the relationship by creative behavior.

We are forced to ask, What kind of child of God should I be? While it is true that fallen humans have often used their creative powers in the pursuit and service of evil, we need to remember that every talent comes from God. The source is divine. God does not restrict our usage of what He has given us. Our responsibility is to glorify the Giver, not the receiver. But the choice remains with the gifted one.

Paul counseled the believers at Ephesus to "be imitators of God" (Eph. 5:1). Thus to live life creatively is to live as God designed human life. C. S. Lewis puts the matter in perspective: "I am uncomfortable with creativity because only God does that. We in our creaturely derivative way are makers; all creativity ultimately derives from God, and we use it in an accommodating sense; God is the only true, unique Creator."

This unnerving reminder reverts to the mystery of the holy Creator residing in the life of a fallen human being. But the ultimate miracle is that we are His most fully developed creatures, *created in His divine image*. That freights us with staggering responsibilities to cultivate and "take care" of His garden (Gen. 2:15). The command to "subdue" (1:28) means "to put to use for My purposes." To "have dominion" (1:28, KJV) is the equivalent of "I am in charge." We are His stewards, His managers, held responsible for the outcome.

Management implies work, an unavoidable component of most lives. Of course, our human nature tends toward extremes—either too much or too little. Obedience to God always attracts the enemy. So it is natural for us to take a good thing like work and twist it ever so slightly, so that it misses the target toward which it was aimed. Recall the notorious Tower of Babel (Gen. 11), a remarkably creative architectural project of the ancient world. Yet its objective was skewed to glorify man, rather than God. Thus He scuttled the venture with the confusion of tongues.

Work has a dual purpose: to continue the process of creation (2:15) and to counter the consequences of sin (3:17–19, 23). The way you think about God influences the way you think about yourself. Thus we will be Godlike in our work if we recognize it as an assignment from Him. As Eugene Peterson put it, "The original task of tending the garden was not abrogated by the Fall, but it was certainly complicated by the thorns and thistles."[8]

Frequently we subvert the intent of creation by using other people, ideas, and material for selfish purposes. Our world evaluates work primarily in terms of productivity; God designated work as creative activity. Buckminster Fuller suggested that the basic purpose of people on earth is to counteract the tide of entropy. That is why he urged, "Dare to be naive." Disorder contradicts every aspect of our God. Quality work performed with a glad heart should be characteristic of God's children. A noncreative Christian is really an oxymoron, an absurd contradiction.

That God is the Master Craftsman and we are the extension of His creative model compels us to contemplate His lavish endowments. We are only a grain of sand before the ocean of His omniscience. God creates *ex nihilo*, out of nothing. We cannot. Only the materials He has created are at our disposal. We simply rearrange the elements He has provided. There is, therefore, a similarity, not an identity, in our creative ability. Thus we are misled if we think our creativity is purely original.

Again note the words of C. S. Lewis. "He seems to do nothing of Himself which He can possibly delegate to His creatures. He commands us to do slowly and blunderingly what He could do perfectly and in the twinkling of an eye. . . . Perhaps we do not fully realize the problem, so to call it, of enabling finite free wills to coexist with omnipotence. It seems to involve at every moment almost a sort of divine abdication."[9]

The Nature of Our Salvation

"The created world, however, has lost its sacredness. Christians have abandoned it, not to paganism, but to physics, geology, biology and chemistry. We have cleaved nature from its superstructure."[10]

Despite the evidence that the universe was created, many people insist on questioning its origin, persist in doubting the evidence, and stubbornly affirm their own authority—against all historical and scientific evidence. Why this perverse refusal to give God credit for what He has so exquisitely done?

The question marks dissolve before the blinding truth of God's written Word. He has demonstrated His power in the natural world; He has imaged Himself in human beings; He has revealed His heart through His inspired revelation. The complete message of who, what, how, and why has been delivered. God has spoken. He started the process of creativity, and He delegated the ongoing work to His creatures. People, like God, are creators. As Dorothy Sayers commented, "The characteristic common to God and man is the desire and ability to make things."[11]

The Creator's handiwork surrounds us. His power in nature astounds us. We know that He has spoken. "Something drastic, something humanly irretrievable happened to the image of God in us when Adam and Eve rebelled against the Creator's command,"[12] Frank Gaebelein reminds us. The soul of man has become septic, separated from God's holiness. To recall Paul's words to the Romans, "Since the creation of the world God's invisible qualities—His eternal power and divine nature—have been clearly seen, being understood from what has been made, so that men are without excuse. . . . Their thinking became futile and their foolish hearts were darkened" (Rom. 1:20–21).

This toxicity level placed humanity on the death roster, doomed to eternal damnation. Nothing is quite as unoriginal as sin. There are no innovative ways to sin. Conversely, the Holy Spirit is inventive and the forms of grace are not repeated.

In our childish imaginations we can almost picture the throngs of angels and heavenly beings watching breathlessly the tragedy in the Garden, then turning toward the Trinity with a corporate question, "*Now what are You going to do?*" Adam and Eve, the most eminent and exalted pinnacles and protectors of the grand earthly creation, had used their free will to disobey the holy Father. Now what? Was there any hope for these disobedient children with a God of absolute justice?

The sequel to the drama flows from the pen of Paul with the best news ever announced. There *is* hope! "Hope does not disappoint us, because God has poured out His love into our hearts by the Holy Spirit whom He has given us. You see, at just the right time, when we were still powerless, Christ died for the ungodly. . . . While we were still sinners, Christ died for us. . . . We have been justified by His blood" (Rom. 5:5–8).

Each believer is "a new creation" (2 Cor. 5:17), the ultimate form of interior remodeling. The changes are substantial, not superficial. When a natural person is invaded by the supernatural person of God's Son, a radical alteration in lifestyle is called for. The new plan calls for a new man. Salvation affects all of a person's life, including his mind. Note how often the word *mind* appears in the New Testament—always in the control of God or Satan. Why? Because whoever controls the mind controls the person.

That is why Paul cautioned us, "Do not conform any longer to the pattern of this world, but be transformed by the renewing of your mind" (Rom. 12:2). Renewal is a lifelong process, a systemic refresher course needed by each new generation. Ray Ortlund reminds us, "We should not think, 'Well, of course, we have the gospel.' . . . Such complacency will cost us dearly. Every generation of Christians must be retaught afresh the basic truths of our faith. The church is always one generation away from total ignorance of the gospel. . . . All the treasures of wisdom and knowledge are hidden in Christ. If we do not intentionally search them out, we will miss them."[13]

A cleansed imagination is one of the by-products of a regenerated intellect. It's a thinking capability, an imagination, released from its prison of the ordinary and liberated to become what God redeemed us to be.

Consider how profoundly powerful that can be. The United States went to the moon not primarily because of the technology of its citizens but because of their imagination.

"Where the Spirit of the Lord is, there is freedom. The letter kills, but the Spirit gives life" (2 Cor. 3:17). Not legalism, but liberty. In light of this truth, we must ask ourselves, Does our ministry kill or liberate?

God does not love us on a performance basis. Lewis Sperry Chafer, founder of Dallas Theological Seminary, used to assure his students, "Nothing you will ever do will cause God to love you more; nothing you will ever do will cause Him to love you less." This divine love, this incomprehensible grace, reveals the secret of humanity's accomplishments.

Before Jesus died on the cross, He promised His disciples, "Anyone who has faith in me will do what I have been doing. He will do even greater things than these. . . . You may ask me for anything in my name, and I will do it" (John 14:12–14). What an astounding confidence-builder for the believer!

The Nature of Our Calling

If God is who He says He is, if we humans are who He says we are, and if He has secured us as believers for salvation from hopelessness and uselessness, as He says He has, then that implies an assignment, a calling—one that opens personal doors of expression with unlimited possibilities. Not only that, but also the Lord has come in person to give us a "multimedia demonstration" of how our lives should be lived.

One of the most pervasive and staggering concepts in the New Testament is the incarnational principle. To an infinite God, there are conceivably inexhaustible ways in which He might have chosen to communicate with humanity. He chose Incarnation. "The Word became flesh and lived for a while among us. We have seen his glory, the glory of the one and only Son who came from the Father, full of grace and truth" (John 1:14). "The Son is the radiance of God's glory and the exact representation of his being, sustaining all things by his powerful word" (Heb. 1:3).

God's method is to clothe truth with personality. He strategizes ministry by taking a clean person and dropping him into the midst of a corrupt society to demonstrate what His grace can produce in human experience. We call it modeling, which Professor Albert Bandura of Stanford University has called the greatest form of unconscious learning.

"A saint is one who exaggerates what the world neglects."

—G. K. Chesterton

Think about it: Jesus was born in an unpredictable way; He lived an unforgettable life; He died an unspeakable death. Jesus never used the same approach twice in His evangelistic or teaching ministry. Innovative diversity was His style. And if we allow Him to teach us, we will become like Him in our generation.

Jesus' approach was always determined by the real needs of the people and their individual requirements. He ate with tax collectors and prostitutes, invited women to be close companions in His work, touched lepers, and devoted gentle words to little children. He was unrestricted by the straitjacket of public opinion. No sameness, monotony, or mass production ever marked His methods, even though His ministry was broad-based to thousands of people. He assumed nothing, but He questioned everything for the benefit of each individual soul.

Thus Jesus modeled a genuinely creative life for us. To quote Eugene Peterson again, "Truly creative people are not connoisseurs who walk through the art galleries of the world, collecting the finest works, but those who involve themselves in the stuff of the world and make the best pictures."[14]

In his excellent book *Game Plan*, Bob Buford reminds us with keen insight of what we so often forget: "I have found that many people are really afraid of Christianity because they think it is all about uniformity and conformity, whereas it doesn't take much observation to see that the plan of creation is not one of conformity but of endless diversity."[15]

Allowing Christ to infuse our service for Him requires an imagination that is fully alert. Cheryl Forbes advised us to awaken our imaginations and wake up to life. "What often passes for creativity is merely bad art, bad craft, bad ideas. It happens because imagination is left out. . . . What may help us see is that any life, no matter how ordinary, is extraordinary with God. He shattered ordinariness with the incarnation. We just haven't got the message yet."[16]

Having been commissioned to express our distinctiveness with the dynamic of Jesus' life in us and His example before us, we must train ourselves to discern not only good from evil but also the elegant from the ugly, the profitable from the pretentious. Again, Carl F. H. Henry points out that the soul of modern man has been sucked dry by temporary concerns that eclipse the eternal world. Our efforts are sentenced to futility unless we are fortified with creative ideas, the only prevention against being victimized by the worthless ones.

Creativity for the Christian, then, stands solidly on a four-legged stool supported by the nature of our God, His imprint etched on us as His creatures, His rescue from our slippery slope of dull monotony, and His stimulating challenge to us, complete with built-in fulfillment. Of all the people in the world, those who have been transformed through allegiance to Christ have the best rationale for creative endeavor.

"Live creatively, friends. . . . Make a careful exploration of who you are and the work you have been given, and then sink yourselves into that. Don't live vicariously. Each of us must take responsibility for doing the creative best we can with our own lives."[17]

Exercises

1. Use a concordance to do word studies on words related to creativity in the Bible: for example, *create, created, make, made, form, fashion.*
2. Read Psalm 104. Then list all the ways in which God reveals His creativity through creation.
3. Read Psalm 8:3–8. In light of what you have seen in Psalm 104, what do you think it means for human beings to be "ruler over the works of [God's] hands" (8:6)? How do you think that rule relates to creativity?
4. Read Exodus 31:1–11 and 35:30–36:1. What was the source of

these artisans' creativity? How did their creativity enable them to contribute to the building of the tabernacle?

5. Think about your own abilities. In what ways do you display creativity? What do you suppose is the source of these creative powers? If your creativity is from God, what does that mean for the way you exercise your talents, and how you develop them?

Helpful Resources

- Forbes, Cheryl. *Imagination: Embracing a Theology of Wonder.* Portland, Oreg.: Multnomah Press, 1986.
- O'Connor, Elizabeth. *Eighth Day of Creation.* Waco, Tex.: Word, 1971.
- Richmond, Gary. *A View from the Zoo.* Waco, Tex.: Word, 1987.
- Ryken, Leland. *Culture in Christian Perspective.* Portland, Oreg.: Multnomah, 1986.
- *The Wonder of God's Creation.* Videotape series, available from Moody Bible Institute, 820 North LaSalle Street, Chicago, IL, 60610. Especially useful are the films on the animal kingdom, planet earth, and human life.

Kinds of Creative Thinking

From the cowardice that dares not face new truth, from the laziness that is contented with half-truth, from the arrogance that thinks it knows all truth, Good Lord, deliver me. Amen.

—PRAYER FROM KENYA

4

Creative behavior begins in the brain of a thinking individual with a desire to cause constructive change. Since human life will always present problems, new solutions will always be needed. For example, if I were to break my right arm, that would pose a substantial creative challenge. I would need to think creatively about how to reorganize my life to accommodate the loss. That would require activating parts of my body in some new ways, and possibly using some new techniques, in order to meet my needs.

Thus creativity involves thinking. And as an art, thinking produces either pain or pleasure. Unfortunately too many people assume that when they become Christians, they are obligated to commit intellectual suicide. Yet nothing could be further from the truth. At least, from biblical truth.

A sign in a business office reads, "You are not what you think you are. What you *think*, you *are!*" That's actually a rather biblical perspective. "As a man thinketh in his heart, so is he" (Prov. 23:7, KJV).

Therefore we need to allow Christ to transform our minds as well as our hearts. Recall that the Great Commandment is to love the Lord our

God with all our heart, soul, *and mind* (Matt. 22:37). Likewise, Paul informed us that spiritual transformation involves a process of "renewing" our *mind* (Rom. 12:2). Elsewhere the apostle counseled, "Brothers, stop *thinking* like children. In regard to evil be infants, but in your *thinking* be adults" (1 Cor. 14:20, italics added). And again, "We take captive every *thought* to make it obedient to Christ" (2 Cor. 10:5, italics added).

So how are you loving God with your *mind?* Let me suggest four kinds of creative thinking by which you can do that.

Dual Thinking

Roger W. Sperry, psychologist at the California Institute of Technology, won the Nobel Prize in 1981 for his groundbreaking research on the human brain. Corroborative study since Sperry's original work is overwhelming, revealing how we can use our brain's incredible potential for personal growth.

One of the key discoveries is the dual nature of human thinking. The human brain is designed with two hemispheres, left and right. Generally speaking, the left hemisphere controls verbal and analytical processes, and the right hemisphere controls visual and perceptual processes. This takes us back to the question of loving God with our mind. We need to love Him with *both* sides of our brain!

The biblical writers certainly did. For example, the Book of Romans illustrates left-brain activity. It is analytical and inductive. Proverbs, on the other hand, is more of a right-brain book—poetic and picturesque. (To be fair, both hemispheres of the brain had to have been employed in writing the Scriptures; but it's interesting to consider that one or the other side tends to dominate, as shown by the end product.)

Betty Edwards has written a fascinating explanation of right-mode thinking, in which she provides a helpful chart to distinguish the two hemispheres.[1]

A Comparison of Left-Mode and Right-Mode Characteristics of the Brain

LEFT MODE	RIGHT MODE
Verbal: Using words to name, describe, define.	*Nonverbal:* Awareness of things, but minimal connection with words.
Analytic: Figuring things out step by step and part by part.	*Synthetic:* Putting things together to form wholes.
Symbolic: Using a symbol to stand for something (e.g., the + sign stands for the process of addition).	*Concrete:* Relating to things as they are at the present moment.
Abstract: Taking out a small bit of information and using it to represent the whole thing.	*Analogic:* Seeing likenesses between things; understanding metaphoric relationships, comparisons.
Temporal: Keeping track of time, sequencing one thing after another. Doing first things first, second things second.	*Nontemporal:* Without a sense of time.
Rational: Drawing conclusions based on reason and facts.	*Nonrational:* Not requiring a basis of reason or facts; willingness to suspend judgment.
Digital: Using numbers, as in counting.	*Spatial:* Seeing where things are in relation to other things and how parts go together to form a whole.
Logical: Drawing conclusions based on logic: one thing following another (e.g., mathematical theorem or a well-stated argument).	*Intuitive:* Making leaps of insight often based on incomplete patterns, hunches, feelings, or visual images.
Linear: Thinking in terms of linked ideas, one thought directly following another, often leading to a convergent conclusion.	*Holistic:* Seeing whole things all at once; perceiving the overall patterns and structures, often leading to divergent conclusions.

While the left brain is primarily critical and the right brain creative, evidence is accumulating that creativity demands using both sides of the brain to work together synergistically, producing a vast array of combinations.

Through education, environment, and experiential factors, Westerners tend to develop more as left-brained than as right-brained individuals. This conditioning greatly hampers our ability to think creatively. So any attempt we can make to strengthen our right brain's capacity is a significant step to developing our creative potential.

Edwards outlines a strategy for making a left-to-right cognitive shift. First, in order to gain access to the subdominant, visual, perceptual, right-mode of the brain, it is necessary to present the brain with a job that the verbal, analytical left-mode will turn down. Conversely, to access the verbal, analytical left-mode, it is necessary to present the brain with a task appropriate to the left-mode rather than the right (such as reading, writing, or arithmetic, for example).[2]

Edwards proposes techniques for preventing the logical, verbal left brain from blocking off creative visions of the pictorial right brain. She suggests encouraging yourself to direct your attention toward visual information that the left brain cannot or will not process.

The two exercises on the facing page will enable you to practice using the creative visions of the pictorial right brain rather than the logical and verbal left brain.

An everyday example of these exercises is the increasing use of graphic, iconic signs in public places to provide directions and warnings. For readers (left-brain), who are accustomed to printed text, these pictures require the use of the other side of their brains in order to grasp the meaning. (See Exercise One.)

Another technique Edwards recommends is to draw the outline or profile of a face. (See Exercise Two.) Then draw the face in reverse or mirror image; that is, facing the first one. By placing horizontal lines at the top (or forehead) and bottom (or chin), the drawing takes the shape of a vase.

Changes in cognitive thinking occur with how one thinks about the shape. As one is drawing, he should be naming the parts of the face. This naming of symbolic shapes is right-brain thinking. In the reverse drawing process, the comparison, measuring, and estimating of distances is a left-brain function.

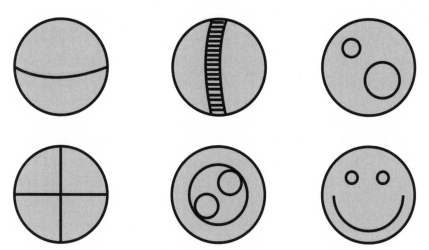

Exercise One—Work out three interpretations for each shape.
(Source: Tom Wujec, *Five Star Mind*)

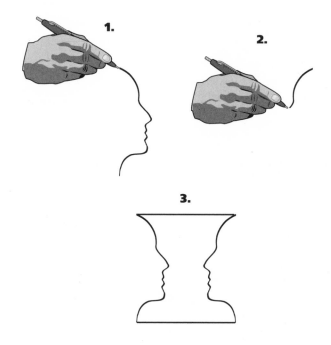

Exercise Two

Both brain hemispheres, however, are vital. Each complements the other and makes it more productive. When the two hemispheres work cooperatively, they can produce new and sensible solutions to almost any problem a person wishes to explore.

Here are some additional suggestions for developing both sides of the brain:

1. Learn the specialized functions of each hemisphere, so that you can complement the mode best suited to the appropriate task.

2. Assign tasks that demand the use of the neglected mode. For example, if you sense you are deficient in left-brain thinking, use assignments that demand writing or speaking. To develop your right brain, use diagramming, painting, or composing a song or riddle.

3. Vary your style of parenting or teaching. For example, resist answering questions with labels. Use more explorations than explanations. Employ touching, smelling, comparing, imagining, listening, and viewing an object from different angles so that life becomes fascinating and complex, not boring and predictable.

4. Provide plenty of materials (chalk, paints, paper, crayons) with which to express ideas imaginatively. Drawing is an excellent way to employ one's creative juices. Indeed, all the arts can stimulate creativity.

5. Identify your most effective way of learning—which is not necessarily the way you were "taught" to learn. Remember, the brain requires different kinds of tools if it is to grow.

Ample evidence supports the idea that the right side of the brain is especially skilled at creative innovation. The problem? Most of our right brains have been so completely dominated by the logical, unimaginative left-brain thinking of our Western world that our right brain needs to be unleashed.

Too much of our thinking is reflexive, rather than reflective. It is also increasingly subject to computerized decisions. Many movers and shakers are among us, but we have an unbelievably short supply of meditative and contemplative thinkers.

Why is it that we have glorified the relatively undisciplined, chaotic phase of the creative process and almost ignored the disciplined, law-seeking, form-imposing side of creativity? Today we fear the judging, critical mind; tolerance is the "in" word. Yet we cannot avoid the necessity of using our minds to make judgments. It is not a matter of choice—whether you are a parent, teacher, programmer, pilot, weatherman, policeman, CEO, politician, or physician. Choices are the inevitables of life. Thus the mind is an instrument of soaring possibilities, but also of depraved limitations. It is capable of both brilliance and stupidity.

As we have noted, the left brain is primarily critical, the right brain is primarily creative. This is not to say one side is better than the other. *Both* parts of our divinely designed thinking machine are essential. But it is important for us to recognize that the two sides differ—and that most of us use only half of what we've got!

Divergent Thinking

The ability to discover alternatives to a given idea is another capability of the right side of our creative brains. Historian Alfred North Whitehead defined this facility of divergent thinking as "the effective utilization of knowledge."

Here's an exercise to illustrate the principle of divergent thinking:

Form a group of six people, one of whom is not aware of the purpose of the exercise. Draw two lines (as shown), one of which is slightly, but not obviously, longer than the other. The five informed ones in the group should declare that the two lines are equal. In all likelihood the sixth member will protest loudly. Over time, however, the pressure of the group will invariably convince the sixth that his eyesight is declining.

Forms of this exercise have been employed in scientific research. The results dramatically demonstrate what happens with peer pressure—at all ages. A person may insist on living differently, breaking from the herd; but over time he tends to capitulate and go along with those around him.

For thinking Christians, this tendency toward the mean can be lethal. That's why Paul urged us, "Do not allow the world to squeeze you into its mold" (Rom. 12:2, PHILLIPS). Unfortunately we are not developing many people in the Christian community who are capable and committed to critical thinking, because they have not become *divergent* Christian thinkers. People of any age tend to cave in to peer pressure unless they are confident in a countercultural posture. But if they have that confidence, they can become aware of their options and know when and how to take a stand.

This is one reason we Christians need to be aware of our opposition— to know what we are up against. Debate is an excellent training ground for developing this kind of thinking, and we do well to find sparring partners or a wide-awake discussion group. It also helps to read informed data about the ideas put forth by our opponents.

Scripture is filled with passages in which the need for divergent thinking is critical. For example, consider the radical implications of these words of Jesus: "Blessed are the meek, for they will inherit the earth" (Matt. 5:5). "Whoever wants to save his life will lose it" (Mark 8:34–35). "A man's life does not consist in the abundance of his possessions" (Luke 12:15).

How different these challenges are from the modern bromide "You only go around once in life, so live it up while it lasts!" Or, "You can be anything you want to be." (Here is where the technique of Objection-Countering is useful; see chapter 12.)

Conservative Christians are often charged with the weakness of being resistant to change. The deeper concern is, In what area? Truth, or a distorted perception of the truth? Admittedly our mentality as evangelicals is often not conducive to creativity. This is true for at least two reasons. First, we tend to like simple, packaged ideas that have closure and uniformity. After all, we reason, Paul told the Philippians to be "like-minded"

(Phil. 2:2; 4:2). However, being of the same mind does not always mean being of the same opinion.

Second, we have a persistent dislike of tension, opposition, open-ended ideas, ambiguity, and mystery. Yet again, note the teaching of Scripture: "Now we see but a poor reflection as in a mirror; then we shall see face to face. Now I know in part; then I shall know even as I am fully known" (1 Cor. 13:12). Our finite minds simply cannot comprehend infinite truth. So perhaps we do not appreciate the company we are in. Are we not pleased to share the realism of Paul?

Deliberate Thinking

A further essential for creative thinking is the willingness to be consciously intentional in our approach to an assignment. This purposeful way of thinking is conscious and deliberate in contrast to blind, undisciplined, and scattered thoughts. It involves the calculated development of creative behavior and human potential.

Maria Montessori, in her pivotal book *The Absorbent Mind*, claimed this is the way all children begin thinking.[3] They are endowed with a ravenous collection of blotter-like, hungry senses. Yet all too easily, their appetites for learning are lost through individuals who fail to cooperate with the Lord's built-in creativity development program.

Someone has said that 75 percent of Americans never think; 15 percent think they think but really only rearrange their prejudices; leaving only 10 percent who really think! These thinking people—the remnant, as it were—are the truly valuable members of any organization or society. We need more of them in the church.

We find a charter for Christian thought in Philippians 4:8–9. Paul concluded his counsel with the imperative, "*Think about* such things" (italics added). The Jerusalem Bible translates this, "Fill your mind with these things." Six categories are suggested with which to fill and nourish our minds: things that are true, noble, right, pure, lovely, and admirable. One commentator proposes that the things that are "true" may well be the one essential that governs the qualities that follow. What an enriching curriculum for intentional thinking!

When we consider the fact that Hugh Hefner, founder of *Playboy* magazine, and Harold John Ockenga, eminent seminarian and Bible expositor, were products of the same church youth group, we are forced to ask, What happened to produce such radically different outcomes? Perhaps one was merely *exposed* to truth, while the other *experienced* it. How deliberate were their leaders in developing the creative potential of these two young men, while at the same time attempting to imbue their minds with eternal truth?

What is needed is creative calisthenics, for two reasons: first, to develop an individual's creative muscles through designed exercises, and second, to prevent the atrophying of the human mind.

This principle is best demonstrated in the physical realm. The mind is like a muscle: It grows with usage, it atrophies with disuse. Muscles do not develop automatically without a planned program. As with an athlete, if you don't practice, your mind grows flabby and out of shape.

Likewise, creativity is rarely produced spontaneously. There are processes that can help increase the likelihood of creative ideas and behavior. They will not make them happen, but they will multiply the probability. I once asked a well-experienced pathologist friend, "Have you ever seen a brain that's worn out?" "Hendricks," he chuckled, "I've never seen one slightly used!"

So run the risk of wearing out your brain!

Creative people are always working at the process. Here's a suggestion: On a sheet of paper write a subject at the top. It doesn't matter what topic you pick. Then, without any input from others, write down everything that comes to your mind about that subject. In time, your thoughts will expand and ripen. Indeed, you may have the beginnings of a good talk or article. Thoughts mature as they pass over the lips and through the fingertips. The key is consciously launching the process.

Deferred Thinking

Deferred thinking is not the same as not thinking. It is not refusing to think but rather postponing the outcome of the process until one has considered every option. It requires one to develop a high tolerance for ambiguity, unanswered questions, and tension. The biblical terms *patience* and *wait* come to mind. If you require everything to which you are exposed to be tied up in neat packages with fancy bows, you will marginalize your creative ability.

Deferred judgment gives the imagination priority over judgment in the early stages of generating ideas. For a spiritual parallel, compare the parable of the weeds (Matt. 13:24–30) in which our Lord warns against pulling weeds prematurely. Sometimes we are too quick to weed the gardens of our minds, with the result that we pull up the tender shoots of imaginative ideas before they've had a chance to bloom and bear fruit.

The research on deferred thinking is impressive. Here is a revealing study of the value and productivity of this kind of creativity:

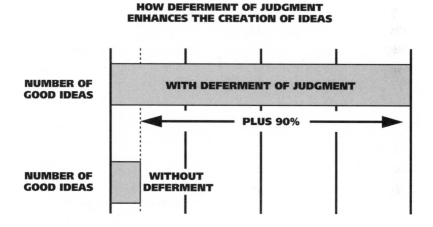

The Pharisees of Jesus' day were clearly disturbed that He upset most of their conventional categories. Overly committed to systems and structure, they were incapable of thinking outside their traditional boxes, and unwilling to live with unanswered questions. Are you like that?

Deferred thinking is the difference between open- and closed-mindedness. Many of us have a tendency to grasp the first idea that comes to mind in order to reduce anxiety. But in the early stages of the creative process, the issue is not, *Is it right or wrong?* but *Where will it take you?* There must be a willingness to play mentally with any concept or idea.

That's not to suggest that you have no convictions. It means you are willing to delay your conclusions until you have examined all the presenting evidence. Thus deferred thinking leads, not to less conviction, but to greater confidence in the conviction you have.

I sometimes wonder if we are not answering too many questions rather than questioning more answers. Our goal should be to develop people who are "prepared to give an answer for the hope that is in them" (1 Pet. 3:15). Premature judgmental thinking kills 90 percent of creative thinking.

MENTAL POWERS

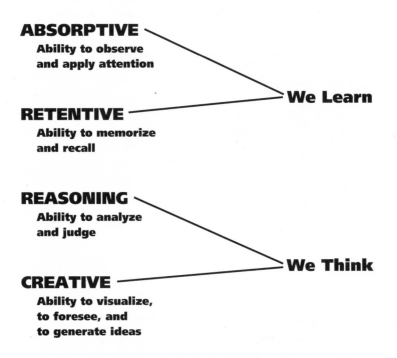

ABSORPTIVE
  Ability to observe
  and apply attention

RETENTIVE
  Ability to memorize
  and recall

We Learn

REASONING
  Ability to analyze
  and judge

CREATIVE
  Ability to visualize,
  to foresee, and
  to generate ideas

We Think

The Genius of the "And"

A landmark book appeared in 1994, entitled *Built to Last*, by James C. Collins and Jerry I. Porras.[4] This should be required reading for every Christian leader, professional or lay, because it represents six years of intensive research that identifies crucial factors that drive successful visionary companies.

What separates the bronze, silver, and gold medalists among the world's great corporations? Collins and Porras highlight four key principles, all of which are applicable and essential to the church. But two are especially relevant to the subject of creativity. The first can be described as "the tyranny of the 'or' versus the genius of the 'and.'"

The authors claim that we live in a society that is brutalized by the tyranny of the "or"—the assumption that you always have to choose between A *or* B, this *or* that, short-term *or* long-term, favoring management *or* favoring workers, making money *or* serving a higher purpose, and so on.

The genius of the "and," however, is a rejection of the "or" in favor of the view that says, "We're going to figure out ways to have A *and* B, this *and* that, short-term *and* long-term." The idea is to put the "ands" together, to combine seemingly contradictory things in creative ways that actually turn out better than they would have working apart.

Recall our earlier discussion about dual thinking and divergent thinking, and you begin to see the genius of the "and." Specific illustrations that apply to the Christian setting might include the following:

- Praying *and* planning (see Neh. 1 and 2)
- Trusting God *and* exercising human initiative (see Col. 1:28–29)
- Quality teaching *and* aggressive evangelism (Acts 2:41–47)
- Studying Scripture *and* studying the culture (1 Chron. 12:32)
- Faith *and* work (see Romans and James)
- Christian growth both internal *and* external
- Doctrinal purity *and* cultural relevance
- Professional clergy *and* laypeople (see Eph. 4)

The Christian community is often fractured because it suffers from the tyranny of the "or." We divide over secondary issues, when in reality we need both. This causes us to move in the direction of extremes.

Preserve the Core

A second key principle Collins and Porras identified in organizations that last is the centerpiece to the entire creative process. It is this: "Preserve the core, and stimulate progress." The core is understood as a philosophical, ideological set of values; in a word, your purpose. Core values answer the question, Why are we in existence?

Core values never change; they are a fixed stake in the ground that informs the world, "This is why we exist. This is what we stand for. We hold these truths to be self-evident." They are not really open for change. They are fanatically preserved and embedded into the organization.

Yet simultaneous with this loyalty to the core, enduring organizations always stimulate themselves toward progress. They show a willingness— indeed, an intentionality—to develop and change everything else *but* the core values.

This is the paradox of creativity for Christians. We live and minister in a society that is pervasively and constantly changing, but eternal verities must not be compromised. In other words, we must determine what cannot change and what must change. Knowing the difference enables us to progress, because knowing what should not change releases us to be open to alternatives in other areas. Values and practices must be aligned.

This insight of Collins and Porras is profoundly significant, but it can make evangelicals uncomfortable because all too often we do not know the difference between what cannot be changed and what must be changed. We are chronically confusing the biblical and the cultural. Result? We tend to dilute what should never be changed and fail to upgrade what must be changed. Moreover, we are often doing what any other human organization can do but not doing what only the church can do. We become easily distracted and detour from our biblical mandate.

Every Christian organization I've ever seen has practices that are considered sacred that I am convinced are not. That poses a challenge: Do we know our core values and core purpose so that we can differentiate between what we will preserve and what we will keep open for change? How rigorously clear are we? Perhaps we are not as clear as we should be.

Be fanatical about preserving the core, but at the same time be very intentional about reevaluating priorities. The message of Scripture never changes; the methodology of communicating that message in our generation must change.

Until these two principles—the genius of the "and" and preserving the core while stimulating process—are clearly understood and wedded, we will continue to blunder in the process of developing creativity in our churches and our personal lives. Conversely, it is totally possible to honor our Founder's purpose and still operate in a contemporary society. We can, as Paul wrote, be "all things to all men" (1 Cor. 9:22) if we are willing to balance these two critical concepts. But if we ignore either one, we do so at our own peril.

Exercises

1. Complete the following sequences:
   a. 2, 4, 6, 8, _____
   b. fun/run, rat/cat, speak/peak, show/_____
   c. 3, 7, 15, 31, _____
   d. purple, blue, green, yellow, _____
   e. roots are to trees as tires are to cars

      wings are to birds as sails are to ships

      sunlight is to the earth as water is to _____
   f. star, light, space, time, _____
   • Which of the sequences is most difficult? Why?
   • Which took you the longest time to complete?
   • Which side of your brain do you think is required by each of the sequences?
2. Add only one straight line to make the following true:

5 + 5 + 5 = 550

3. Divide the pizza below into eight pieces using only three lines:

4. Plexars are illustrations that symbolically represent words or phrases. See if you can decipher what the following plexars mean:

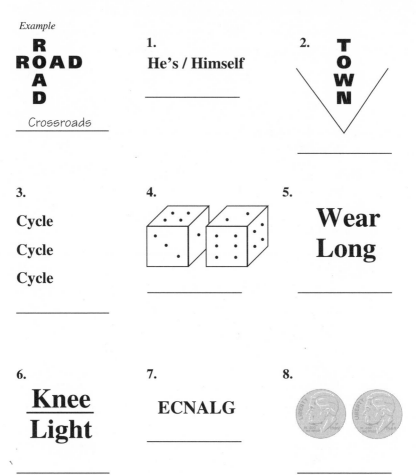

Example

R
ROAD
A
D

Crossroads

1.

He's / Himself

_____

2.

T
O
W
N

_____

3.

Cycle

Cycle

Cycle

_____

4.

_____

5.

Wear

Long

_____

6.

Knee
Light

_____

7.

ECNALG

_____

8.

_____

5. Name one thing to which you are willing to devote *deliberate thinking* during the next four weeks. Write that subject on a 3" x 5" card or a Post-It note and place it where you will be reminded of it regularly. Also, reserve a set amount of time in your schedule or appointment book *each day* for the next month for devoting thought to that topic. At the end of the four weeks, ask yourself the following questions:

- What happened through the process of focusing attention on this topic? What happened to the topic? What happened to me as a result of my thinking about the topic?
- How difficult was it for me to stick to my regimen of deliberate thinking?
- What would I do differently to improve my process of deliberate thinking the next time?
- What other topics could stand to receive my attention through deliberate thinking? How will I make that happen?

6. Read Romans 14. What would be a matter of conscience for you, one where you disagree with other people who hold a different opinion? How could you use the process of deferred thinking on this issue?

7. If you are the leader of a church or organization, consider a discussion with the core members of your group around the ideas raised by Jim Collins and Jerry Porras in *Built to Last*. For example:
   - What are our core values?
   - What is our core purpose?
   - In what ways are we victims of the "tyranny of the 'or'"? How could we move to the "genius of the 'and'"?
   - What are some things that will/should never change about our group?
   - What are some things that need to change and progress?
   - What do we envision for our future?

(Note: Answers to these exercises can be found on page 241.)

Helpful Resources

- Gardner, Howard. *Frames of Mind: The Theory of Multiple Intelligences*. New York: HarperCollins, 1985.
- Moreland, J. P. *Love Your God with All Your Mind*. Colorado Springs: NavPress, 1997.

Characteristics of Creative People

Unless there is an element of risk in the Christian life, there is no need for faith.

—J. HUDSON TAYLOR

5

"Curiosity," observed Samuel Johnson, "is one of the permanent and certain characteristics of a vigorous mind." Certain individuals stand out because they are creatively and constructively inquisitive. Why is it that some people live creatively, but many do not? Is it possible to identify the characteristics of creative individuals in such a way that we can cultivate these traits in our own lives and in the lives of others? The investigations have been extensive and the results impressive.

While this book focuses on the creative process, keep in mind that the process manifests itself in creative persons. So let's direct our zoomer lens on why creativity is more frequent and apparent in some than in others.

> **"The world may change, but true visionaries are always easy to recognize."**
>
> —*Advertisement for Rockwell,* Wall Street Journal, *February 25, 1998*

Many researchers have tried to define the personality of the creative individual, that is, to differentiate the specific qualities that stand out in these people. Why? First, to promote these special distinctions, and second, to recognize the hallmarks and encourage those who have them toward creative pursuits.

Two major approaches have been devised.

- *The holistic,* which attempts to look at the whole personality of a creative person, considering him or her in totality. The assumption is that each individual has a dynamic mix. Following this approach, Abraham Maslow concluded that a creative person is a special kind of human being who has to be considered in his or her entirety, not atomistically. The determinants are in the thousands. Thus there can be no easy road to cultivating creativity.
- *The specific,* which attempts to study the individual ingredients of a creative person. For example, E. Paul Torrence came up with characteristics differentiating highly creative personalities.

In my judgment, a combination of both of these approaches is preferable.

Some societies enhance creativity, while others tend to inhibit it. Silvano Arieti, in his remarkable book *The Magic Synthesis,* spells out nine sociocultural ingredients in the "creativogenic" society:

1. Availability of cultural means
2. Openness to cultural stimuli
3. Stress on becoming, not just on being
4. Free access to cultural media to all citizens without discrimination
5. Exposure to different and even contrasting cultural stimuli
6. Freedom, or even the retention of moderate discrimination, after severe oppression or absolute exclusion
7. Tolerance for diverging views
8. Interaction of significant persons
9. Promotion of incentives and awards.[1]

The implications of these factors for the Christian community are freighted with significance and ought to become a practical set of yardsticks by which to measure the dynamics of our community. Consider the phenomenon among Jews in modern times. For instance, the proportion of Jews awarded the Nobel Prize since 1899 is 28 percent greater than that of the rest of the world's population. Or reflect on the incredible creativity displayed by Jews despite their being forced into ghettoes and Nazi concentration camps. By contrast, many of those who lived under the communist oppression of the former Soviet Union have found it difficult to think independently and creatively.

It must be remembered that an extremely high I.Q. is not a prerequisite for creativity. In fact, the prevailing opinion is that highly intelligent people are not necessarily creative, although many creative people are intelligent. Creativity is a part of, not apart from, what we normally think of as intelligence.

Interestingly, high I.Q. may actually inhibit the inner resources of an individual because self-criticism can become too rigid, or the person learns too quickly what the cultural environment has to offer. Great ability to deduce according to the laws of logic and mathematics makes for disciplined thinkers, but not necessarily for creative people.

Professor Howard Gardner, of the Harvard University Graduate School of Education, has identified seven primary intelligences: language, logic and mathematics, spatial reasoning, music, movement (or bodily kinesthetic), interpersonal, and intrapersonal.[2] He suggests we need to think more comprehensively in terms of these several kinds of intellectual ability that a person may have, rather than just one, namely, the traditional Intelligence Quotient.

The question nags: Can creativity be taught? Or are we born with it? The answer to both questions is yes. A few gifted people are born with creative genius, talents, and motivational drive. But the evidence mounts that in every individual, personal creativeness can be expanded beyond its present level. Genetics plays a part, but so does environment. While some ability may be endowed, more can be developed. Eugene Peterson challenges his readers, "There are vast traits of undeveloped life in most of us. We have capacities for creativity that lie fallow."[3]

Essential Characteristics

The first step in advancing one's creativity is the awareness of what creative people are like. They tend to be individuals marked by these six qualities:

- *Fluency.* Three factors commonly indicate this quality: a fertility of words and ideas; analogical thinking (i.e., the ability to associate);

and a talent of expressing oneself (e.g., as a speaker or actor). This defining quality of fluency appears on almost every list of traits of the creative individual. Many researchers are convinced that this in turn produces the rest of the characteristics below.

- *Flexibility.* The competence in abandoning old ways and initiating new directions demonstrates itself in general spontaneity and specific adaptability.
- *Originality.* This ability produces uncommon responses and unconventional associations as a way of thinking.
- *Redefinition.* This tendency looks at what everyone knows and sees with a specific ability to reorganize and reshape it.
- *Elaboration.* This talent captures two or more abilities for the construction of a more complex object or idea.
- *Sensitivity.* The person with a delicately attuned understanding will see problems and be able to evaluate what needs to be done.

Examining the roots of what causes people to be creative, we find certain essential characteristics that are crucial for the genesis of new ideas. These include the following.

Mental Agility

People with the skill to massage ideas, words, images, concepts, problems, hypotheses, and so on, and who can spot unusual connections between these elements and can scan many options, tend to have greater ability to zero in on one correct choice. This superiority involves a combination of divergent and convergent thinking. Thus one's creativity quotient is measured not by intelligence, but inquisitiveness; not by ability, but agility.

Flexibility

A well-lubricated mental gear shift allows for perspectives from different angles. Most people tend to universalize their experiences. For example, I've encountered well-meaning folks who assume that if God has led them to home-school their children, then of course He intends for *all* Christians to do the same. For these folks, public, private, or Christian schools cease to be live options and are even perceived as out of the will of God. Thus a *personal* choice becomes a *moral* issue.

Flexibility in one's leadership style will depend on the needs of the group. This involves the differences between a leader and a manager. A manager is concerned with doing things right, while a leader focuses on doing the right things. The one is systematic, the other entrepreneurial.

Originality

Uncommon ideas, even rare, weird, or wistful theories, are seeds for a creative harvest. You can tame a wild duck, but you can't teach it to be wild again.

Unfortunately many Christians tend to be copycats, and therefore they limit themselves to only *one way* to teach, to evangelize, to conduct worship, and so forth. The church needs more people willing to get on their knees and ask the Lord, "What do You want us to do to reach this community for Christ—whatever it might take?"

Complexity/Simplicity

Innovative people prefer complexity over simplicity at the beginning of the creative process, not at the end. They want to search for the essence of a problem to be solved. If one settles for the simple answer too soon, it may mean overlooking the more significant aspects of the puzzle and settling for superficial solutions.

Robert Louis Stevenson said, "The art of literature is the art of knowing what to omit." One has no adequate basis for omission until he has a comprehensive grasp of the issues involved.

Enriched Background

Exposure to others who are good models of persistent learning fuels creative energy. Creative children are best developed in creative families, where they learn specific skills and achieve because they are endowed with the assets of self-discipline, intense curiosity, a sense of humor, and consistent productivity. Personal problem-solving and the ability to cope with failure add balance to the realism of creative risk.

Multiple Skills

No single path of personal development hobbles creative persons. They keep learning, growing, and are enriched by contact with skilled and life-long learners. The more enriched the context, the greater the creative potential.

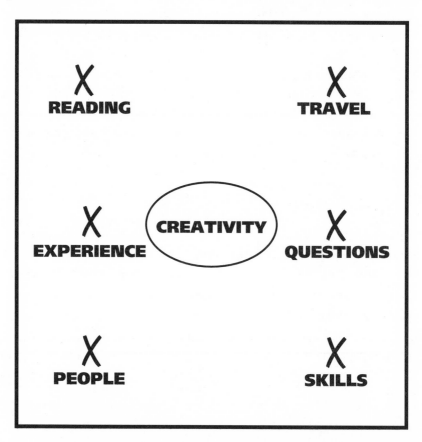

The More Enriched the Context, the Greater the Creative Potential

Risk-Taking

Any creative commitment involves risks. Peter Drucker, father of modern management, reminds us that "risk and security are not in opposition, but parallel." The life of faith is always an experience of stepping into the unknown with our feet firmly planted on the promises of God.

Interestingly, in Jesus' parable of the talents (Matt. 25:14–30), the slave whom the master rebuked was the one who failed to take a risk: "You wicked lazy servant! . . . You should have put my money on deposit with the bankers, so that when I returned, I would have received it back with interest."

So don't be afraid to go out on a limb! That's where the fruit is—and the reward.

> **There was a very cautious man**
> **Who never laughed or played.**
> **He never risked, he never tried,**
> **He never sang or prayed.**
> **And when one day he passed away**
> **His insurance was denied,**
> **For since he never really lived,**
> **They claimed he never died.**

Enabling Characteristics

A number of dynamics can help *keep* the creative process alive.

A Capacity for Hard Work

Soft societies do not produce creative people. As Mark Twain said, "Writing is 10 percent inspiration and 90 percent perspiration." The same percentage applies to other creative activities. In his epistles Paul often used terms of energy such as "toil," "work," "labor," and "striving." Overcoming frustration leads to personal fulfillment. At heart, this is a commitment to excellence—not as compared to others, but to oneself.

Independent Judgment

A strong sense of individuality marks people who make their own decisions and trust their own judgment. Not bowing to group pressure, they maintain self-confidence. As soon as you can express what *you* think, not what someone else has thought for you, you are on your way to becoming a remarkable and totally unique person.

Resilience

Failure is a learning experience. The lesson is, try again! Resist throwing in the towel. Creative winners are positive and realistic. To remind me of this need, I have a plastic Kewpie Doll, weighted on the bottom. Whenever I get frustrated, I bat that thing as hard as I can, trying to knock it flat. But it always lands right side up with a silly little grin on its face!

Similarly, my wife keeps a plastic pyramid on her desk. It is filled with a liquid to resemble the ocean waves. A wind surfer bounces when the "water" moves, but he always stays afloat, no matter the turbulence.

Most people want a guarantee of success. But truly creative individuals will tolerate temporary disorder for the eventual satisfaction of an uncommon result. So be willing to risk and make mistakes. Start on a journey without any control or knowledge of the possible outcome. Don't allow frustration or failure to torpedo you. To take a risk is to be creative.

While visiting Turkey recently, my wife and I were informed that sometimes in the weaving of an Oriental rug, a mistake is made. The rug is not discarded. Instead, Oriental wisdom and imagination combine to incorporate the mistake into an entirely new pattern, often more beautiful than the original. (The American expression for this is, "When life hands you lemons, make lemonade!")

Interest in Concepts More Than Details

This means looking for the big picture. When faced with a new possibility, don't waste time coming up with twenty-five reasons why it won't work. Allow concepts to fascinate you and ignite your after-burners. Unfamiliar concepts should drive your engines!

He failed in business in '31. He was defeated for state legislator in '32. He tried another business in '33. It failed. His fiancee died in '35. He had a nervous breakdown in '36. In '43 he ran for Congress and was defeated. He tried again in '48 and was defeated again. He tried running for the Senate in '55. He lost. The next year he ran for Vice President and lost. In '58 he ran for the Senate again and was defeated again. Finally, in 1860, Abraham Lincoln was elected the 16th president of the United States.

—*Byrd Baggett,* Dare to Soar

Curiosity

Don't just ask, Why? Ask, Why not? Keep your curiosity unquenchable. Nineteenth-century historian Thomas Macaulay once described an acquaintance's imagination as resembling the wings of an ostrich: It enabled him to run, but not to soar. That's tragic! The creative person soars because his curiosity is a thirst never quite slaked.

Bill Hybels, the entrepreneurial pastor of Willow Creek Community Church, South Barrington, Illinois, related in my hearing that as a thirteen-year-old boy he began to hunger for a realistic answer to the question, How can our youth group be structured to attract unchurched teenagers? His persistent curiosity in answering that question ultimately led to the establishment of one of the largest and most effective seeker-driven churches in America.

Playfulness/Spontaneity

Never lose your "play-ability," the fascination of building sand castles on the beach. Be eager to try the untried. Spontaneity never dies in creative people, irrespective of age. It's an attitudinal characteristic.

We are often ready to try the untried when what we do is inconsequential. But some of the most useful inventions have had their birth as toys—the telescope and the microscope, for example. Albert Einstein encouraged us to "pay close attention to the curiosities of a child; this is when the search for knowledge is freshest and most valuable." Perpetuate your ability to play.

Discovering Creative People

Every leader needs to be on the lookout for the creative individuals in his community. They are invaluable resources, because they form a human bridge into the future. How, then, can one spot these imaginative folks?

First, stay alert for people who display the characteristics mentioned above. Keep your antenna up for people who:

- Break with the herd to pursue a meaningful purpose.
- Ask perceptive and penetrating questions such as Why? How? What? and If?
- Are nonconformists and generate original thoughts.

Sadly, our tendency is to run people like this off because they are irregular. But in the process we produce a brain and talent drain.

Second, affirm them in their pursuits. Talented individuals may be accustomed to going against the flow. And their creative juices may flow despite a barren or even hostile environment. But they still need encouragement to sustain their presence and participation. You can help them in these ways:

- Accept and explore their thinking, dreaming, questioning, puttering, studying, reading.
- Give them meaningful assignments, articles to critique, problems to ponder, projects to investigate, questions to answer. Expand their creative boundaries. For example, "Do me a favor. I need help in solving this problem (or finishing this project, or getting ideas for this program)."

Third, involve them in personal mentoring. This form of learning occurs ideally one-on-one, but it can also be effective in groups that are homogeneous and compatible but not devoid of diversity. Remember, discipleship is not a program but a process geared to developing people to their maximum potential (see Col. 1:28–29).[4]

In summary, individuals who behave creatively are those who are oriented toward mining their deeper veins of experience in new ways.

Exercises

1. Use the list of characteristics given in this chapter to evaluate your own creativity quotient.
2. Do you think a high I.Q. is essential to becoming creative? Why or why not? Why do you think people like Albert Einstein, Thomas Edison, and Winston Churchill are so unique?
3. How many people do you know whom you consider to be creative? In each case what indicates their creativity to you? Who are your models of creativity?
4. Recall your childhood memories. Were you more creative then than now? What happened? Why do children tend to be more creative than adults? What causes people to experience an attrition in creative expression?
5. Recall at least one teacher in your educational experience who taught creatively, as you remember it. What were the differences between that teacher and the many others you have forgotten?
6. How important is motivation, and what motivates you to be more creative?
7. Ponder the following three questions:
   - What is your life like right now?
   - What would you like it to be?
   - What are you willing to risk to have that kind of life?

Helpful Resource

- Irwin, Bill, with David McCasland. *Blind Courage*. Dallas: Word, 1992.

Characteristics of a Creative Organization

Have the old Pharisees and the new zealots,
with their conservative and revolutionary
legalism, scared us away from freedom, from joy
and spontaneity?

—JURGEN MOLTMANN

6

"If you continue doing what you are doing, you will get more of what you are getting." That simple truth swims against the tide of our natural thinking. Most of us tend to yield to the centrifugal forces of self-imposed limits, whereas we need to experience a gravitational pull in the direction of creative thinking.

A twofold problem stares menacingly at every Christian organization: One is external (the environment), the other is internal (the individual). However, this double-edged sword can, in reality, be a twin resource, provided we know how to develop creative people. The secret lies in what we see.

To illustrate, think of the difference between a kaleidoscope and an octascope. The kaleidoscopic view is always determined by what is in the cylinder. The more pieces we have in the drum, the more possible patterns we can produce. Similarly in creative learning the greater our collective knowledge, the more patterns, combinations, or ideas we can achieve together. Yet merely having the bits and pieces in the kaleidoscope does not guarantee the formation of new patterns. One must revolve the drum to reveal its beautiful options. We manipulate the knowledge by combining and rearranging facts into new patterns. Whereas a kaleidoscope forms patterns only from what is *within* it, an octascope develops patterns from what is *outside* of it, in the changing environment on which it is focused.

In any organization the combination of external change and internal change produces creative people, ideas, and products. That means that creativity, properly understood, is less interested in inducing any particular change than in fostering the conditions under which constructive, contributory change may occur.

What is it that keeps the spark of curiosity alive in some organizations, that eagerness to learn and the insatiable hunger for experience and life? And how can we rekindle that spark when it flickers out? If we can solve that problem, we are on the verge of a new departure in organizational maturation. Institutions of whatever kind may be so constructed and operated as to enhance or diminish, to liberate or smother, both the individual and the group. Creativity can be stifled or throttled. Therefore we assume a supreme obligation to develop conditions that make creativity possible.

Having examined the marks of creative individuals in the last chapter, it is now our challenging task to shape an arena that is conducive to their growth. Two qualities foster spontaneous and significant results: complete freedom and complete acceptance.

Complete Freedom

What does freedom mean?

First, freedom includes fences and accepts responsibility. One is always free to choose but never free to escape the consequences of those choices. The law of gravity provides a choice illustration. A person is free to jump from a high bridge or a multistory building, but once he is over the railing or out the window, he is no longer free.

Someone complains, "I don't like that law." Well, that law is very insensitive to your feelings. It just functions. "But I don't understand that law," another objects. But that doesn't matter. When the jumper hits the ground, he will have full comprehension! He is bound by the law of gravitation.

Our assignment is to learn the benefits, to get on the good side, of the "law," of the way the world operates. Then we can enjoy our freedom without needing to blame something or someone else for the consequences.

Second, freedom means you have the privilege of being your unique self. Never has there been anyone on the planet like you, and there never will be. Therefore the more you are like yourself, the more distinctive you are. The less you are like anyone else, the more special you are. Furthermore the more you understand who you are, the more you gain insight into others as they are.

One of the most elusive assignments is to get people to be themselves. Invariably they want to be like someone else, because they compare themselves with others rather than developing their own uniqueness. Parents often exacerbate the tendency by reproving, "Johnny, why can't you be like your brother Billy?" The only intelligent answer is, "Because I'm not Billy!"

Comparison in the Christian life is a mark of carnality. King Saul spent his time fighting David rather than the Philistines after he heard the song of the Israelite women: "Saul has slain his thousands, and David his tens of thousands!" (1 Sam. 18:8). Saul's royal pride could not bear such competition; it ate his lunch!

Third, freedom embraces both a positive and a negative component. On the positive side, one must be free for mental exploration—including the freedom to fail. We all fall short, but none of us is a failure unless we fail to learn from our lack of success. Our motto must be: *Nothing to prove, nothing to lose.*

On the negative side, people need to be preserved and protected from the disapproval of others, a withering experience for many. Imagine that a young, eager, aspiring thespian writes and acts in a skit to promote an upcoming Valentine's banquet. The idea is good, but the presentation is amateurish and not well received by the audience.

The raw talent and potential for this young person's future ministry may well be squelched unless she is affirmed as a person and encouraged to learn from the mistakes by going right back and doing it better the next time.

Fourth, freedom requires direction and control. The ceilings of many college chemistry labs bear silent witness to the explosions resulting from combining the wrong ingredients. Likewise many Christians are stained and scarred because two powerful controlling agents—the Scriptures and the Holy Spirit—have been missing (or unbalanced) in their lives and work. The one is propositional, the other personal. If one has too much direction and control, he is hampered from becoming all he is capable of developing. But too little direction results in dangerous eruptions of our sinful natures.

Creative minds in Christian organizations need mentors, disciple-makers, and loving overseers to regulate their priceless supply of talent. The political world graphically demonstrates the dangers involved: Many of those living in Eastern Europe, having been conditioned by seventy years of oppressive control, are now being asked to make independent decisions, sometimes with disastrous results.

Complete Acceptance

What does acceptance mean?

1. Acceptance means respecting individuals for their unconditional worth. Someone has said, "If you accept people as they are, you can become more effective in helping them become better than they are."

2. Acceptance means affirming workers by creating a climate in which external, negative evaluation is minimal. Suppose you have been coaching a reluctant speaker to address an audience, but his attempts are sorely lacking. If you come up with twenty-seven things that are wrong with his presentation, that will seriously demotivate him. Instead, enthusiastically praise three things he has going for him. Then ask, "Would you like to learn something that would make you an even better speaker?"

"Louis Pasteur's theory of germs is ridiculous fiction."

—Pierre Pachet, professor of physiology,
Toulouse University, 1872

3. Acceptance means pursuing empathy and understanding—attempting to see from behind another's eyeballs. By definition creativity means seeing the world from a different perspective—a perspective that differs from yours. The potential for misunderstanding and conflict is great. If you react with fear, hostility, or a heavy-handed attitude of "Hey, cut that out!" you will trample the tender shoots of creativity every time. Instead make things safe for inventiveness to take root. For example, "Wow, Linda, that's something I've never heard before. Tell me more about it."

If we can learn to see through the eyes of others, we may discover new ways of looking at the world—and perhaps even whole new worlds!

Maintaining a Creative Environment

Once we've developed a reasonably safe organizational environment for creativity to flourish, a further question we are compelled to ask is, How do we keep it going? Five flags should be waving.

The Learning-Growing Process

Creative people are lifelong learners. Our task is to motivate that process. Abraham Maslow suggested four levels of learning: unconscious incompetence, conscious incompetence, conscious competence, and unconscious competence.

Once you have completed these steps, you have progressed only halfway. The other half is exposing people to what *keeps* them growing by uncovering information that plunges them to the bottom of the learning ladder. The ultimate test of a church's educational program is not plans and performances but how much people are learning. We tend to impose our agenda from without, rather than encouraging people to develop their own plan from within. As a result, they have difficulty evaluating their lives on the basis of their needs. This outside expectation generates oppression, not ownership.

"What is organizational DNA? It's the stuff, mostly intangible, that determines the basic character of a business. It's bred from the founders, saturates the early employees, and often shapes behavior long after the pioneers have passed on."

—*James F. Moore, "How Companies Have Sex,"*
Fast Company (October/November 1996): 66

A Personal Development Program.

Discipleship programs are often minimally effective because we tend to foist our blueprint on others instead of encouraging them to develop their own. Only a freewill, discretionary plan is workable. Here is a fistful of five keys to that end:

Objectives. Here the question is, What do I want? An increasing number of people who end up at the top of the pile in their field of expertise are at the bottom of life in terms of fulfillment. You achieve that for which you aim; your objectives determine your outcome.

Priorities. What price am I willing to pay? In other words, how badly do I want to accomplish my objectives? Most married couples, for example, want a healthy marriage. But marriage relationships do not happen on the backstroke. Daily cultivation is required.

I once had the privilege of meeting the famous pianist Van Cliburn. I asked him a question I had wondered about for years: "How many hours a day do you practice?" He told me, matter-of-factly, "Six to eight hours—with at least two hours of finger exercises." I then remembered how I once wanted to play the piano—but never *that* badly!

Schedule. What primary means do I have for maintaining my priorities and accomplishing my objectives? To most people, a schedule is a demon chaperone, rapping their knuckles and growling, "Stop that!" In reality, a carefully kept calendar can be a primary tool for managing one's time. The one thing we all have in common is twenty-four hours per day. My schedule is my personal plan to maintain my priorities and accomplish my objectives.

Discipline. What is the dynamic? Every power plant has a means of generating energy—and the control of that energy—if it works efficiently.

For maintaining a positive environment in a creative organization, the Christian's source of regulatory power is the Holy Spirit. If there is any area in which we are out of control, that is proof positive that the Holy Spirit is *not* in control. This quality of self-control is included in the fruit of the Spirit (Gal. 5:22–23), and it separates the men from the boys and the women from the girls.

Evaluation. How am I doing? This aspect of maintenance involves asking and answering four questions: What are my strengths? What are my weaknesses? What needs to be changed? How do I plan to do it?

Here is an area where accountability counts. A caring supervisor needs to request a co-worker to discuss these questions on a regular basis. That builds personal confidence as well as corporate tranquility.

Authentic and Well-Informed Surroundings

Frequently this may require a change of location. I know a pastor whose church sent a group of young couples to the Navigators headquarters in Glen Eyrie near Colorado Springs for one week. The experience not only radically transformed the individuals and their families, but also stimulated them to return to their church with creative ideas for growth. Objectives that he had been striving to attain for years were implemented quickly because of an eight-hundred-mile expedition. That's because a change of location often produces a change of perspective. Informal environments have the highest level of creativity.

Minimal Bureaucracy

Rules and regulations tend to bury creativity. The only rules needed are those that advance the common cause. Anything beyond that is an impediment. Our task is to develop people who do what they do because it makes sense. If the policy is valid, you don't have to force people to do it. Every time an arbitrary policy is instituted, you turn off a little bit more of the faucet of creativity. Policies often communicate the message, "We don't trust you." They are often the product of an outmoded paradigm.

Refusal to Sanction Incompetence

Don't ignore inferior work. Deal with it. How?

- *By determining the level of tolerance.* All of us have to start somewhere; then we flounder in our attempts to improve. But we must improve in order to perform. Consider, for example, the airplane pilot. There's really very little possibility for tolerating a lack of perfection in that occupation. How many times do you want him to land safely? Would ninety-eight or ninety-nine out of one hundred satisfy you? No, it's got to be 100 percent.

That being the case, pilots are allowed mistakes in a Link trainer before they carry passengers. In a similar way we must allow imperfections when people are in a training process, but we must insist on excellence when they are on the job in ministry. For example, when learning to communicate, no one has 100 percent success. It is always a matter of improvement. But we don't take a novice and place him in front of ten thousand people. We graduate his experience. Improvement is the name of the game.

- *By informing and encouraging people when they change for the better.* As an educator, I've seen many students give up because no one ever convinced them, "You are moving toward excellence." There is nothing worse than changing and improving but having no one acknowledge your progress.
- *By teaching people how not to be incompetent.* Churches and Christian organizations should have the motto "No job without training." Help people acquire the skills needed to be successful in whatever they are called to do. Give them a chance to do good work!

Creative Environment Axioms

1. Test your environment as to how it *feels*.
2. Creative people nurture creative people.
3. Crucial question: Are we having *fun?*
4. Talk willingly and openly about failures as being essential to development.
5. Some organizations develop creative people by the bucketful and others do not. Why?

6. Feedback from people within creative Christian organizations:
   - "It's a magic place."
   - "You write your own ticket."
   - "It's a moving target."
   - "Anyone can present an idea to the pastoral staff."
   - "Structured people can't survive here."
   - "There's always something going on."
   - "These people believe they can do anything if God leads them to do it."

7. If you want people to step out, don't share with them your seven decisions.

8. Confess to your people that at times *you* are afraid, have dropped the ball, and have struggled.

9. If you find a room of successful people, the only trait they will share in common is that they have had more failures than their less successful peers.

10. Make ten mistakes a day. If you don't, you are not learning enough.

Exercises

1. In your own life at home, work, church, and leisure, what contributes most to your becoming creative?

2. Would you say you enrich your environments or deplete them? Be specific and objective.

3. What is the value or curse of TV? List both positives and negatives.

4. Think of as many ways as possible to improve the environment of your office, home, or study. For example, use the principles of five-sensing discussed in chapter 11.

5. In what environment are you the most creative? Why? Come up with specific reasons and conclusions.

Helpful Resources

- Collins, James C., and Jerry I. Porras. *Built to Last.* New York: HarperCollins, 1994.
- Bennis, Warren, and Patricia Ward Birderman. *Organizing Genius: The Secrets of Creative Collaboration.* Reading, Mass.: Addison-Wesley, 1997.

The Practice of Creativity

There is great potential in dreams, and the cost is free.

—**Byrd Baggett**

7

Too many Christians have lived too long in a cultural cocoon. We have stretched to extremes the command of our Lord to keep unspotted from the world, often suppressing our natural free-flowing ideas. Chapter 18, "Barriers to Creativity," discusses some specific problems that put a choke hold on us. But for now, we need to recognize that, just as we can throttle our imagination, we can likewise accelerate it.

I have observed that the average person does not trust himself sufficiently to create and deliver new ideas. Most of us worry about inviting ridicule by doing something silly or outlandish. We would rather not venture a new idea than be thought of as absurd. Nevertheless we recognize our need to practice creative behavior. We admit that we are guilty not only of errors of commission but of errors of omission.

"The challenge of keeping creatively alive is analogous to what medicine and other sciences have accomplished in lengthening man's life expectancy and in reducing death at birth," wrote E. Paul Torrance. The active mind, alive with curiosity and an inventive spirit, enriches and expands even a fragile, limited physical life into a powerhouse. One thinks immediately of disabled individuals such as Stephen Hawking or Joni Eareckson Tada, without whom the world would be deeply impoverished. Creativity does not exist in a vacuum; it demands an enriched context with multiple means for increasing one's potential.

Experience

Experience furnishes fuel for ideation, provided it is varied and evaluated. It is the best education because it provides individual instruction. Unfortunately most people live in the past with a museum of memories or in the future with an encyclopedia of expectations. Seldom do people see present, everyday experiences as fertilizer for a creative posture.

Exploding from the pages of Hebrews 11 are creative people who used the ordinary challenges of life to climb above the commonplace. Recall Abel, stubbornly sticking to his convictions about sacrifices, or Noah, persisting in his dry dock because he saw beyond the here and now.

Likewise, Abraham's strange rural itinerary, aged Isaac's and Jacob's blessing their sons, and Joseph's steady progression of promotions in the pagan Egyptian bureaucracy all appeared at the time to be lacking in high drama. But each of these men was plugged into a creative power circuit so that God Himself chose him as an exhibit of how to translate daily events into classic masterpieces for the betterment of future generations.

Think, then, about some of the possible productive triggers in our customary lives:

Travel. This is especially valuable in a culture and location removed from one's normal lifestyle. Travel exposes us to personal contact with those of other ethnicities, customs, age-groups, or philosophies.

Reading. Printed materials and computer-generated data provide endless ideas to increase and enrich us in our information age.

Special occasions. The birth of a child, baptisms, weddings, funerals, and celebrations all supply creative seedlings we can plant for further cultivation.

Reflection. Recalling one's own childhood, earlier triumphs and losses, and growth patterns in unexpected directions can all spark new ideas for the future.

Animals, new opportunities, and seemingly impossible assignments. All these provide grist for the creativity mill.

The aging process should allow us to become more creative as our personal portfolio increases. Experience helps us use each one more profitably. Good judgment comes from living with our eyes open. Learning from evaluated experience is the root definition of the creative life.

Problem-Solving

Chapter 8 examines more closely this fascinating component of creativity. But we include it in our description of the practice of creativity because it is an integral part of everyday living.

Some years ago one of my seminary students was always late to class. It didn't matter whether the class began at 8:00 A.M. or 3:00 P.M. Writing on the chalkboard, my back to the class, I could hear the door open, and instinctively I knew who was slinking in. Inevitably he was exactly seven minutes late—no exception. In fact, at his graduation service he scurried into his seat exactly seven minutes after all his peers were seated!

Later, this same former student invited me to his church for a conference. And yes, you guessed it—every meeting began exactly seven minutes after the announced time! Honestly, I think if it were in his control, he would be seven minutes late for the Rapture! (Not really, but I suspect he would go up dragging his feet!)

"Tackle your troubles" is good counsel. That fellow never did. But he could have, had he bothered to use a little imagination. Every time you solve a problem, you exercise creativity. The unfortunate thing is not that we *have* problems but that we still have the same problems that plagued us ten years ago. Creative minds don't just seek solutions; they also anticipate the difficulties ahead.

Charles Kettering called problem-solving "systematically challenging the obvious." The Book of James counsels us to "count it all joy" when troubles arise. Why? Because we know that "the testing of [our] faith develops endurance" (1:2–3). Useful outcomes grow from rugged circumstances.

Becoming intentionally creative develops question marks in the brain, an insatiable curiosity. How can these quandaries be resolved? What alternative can I find to escape this cul-de-sac or to bridge this gap? Even games, puzzles, chess, and the like contribute to skills in problem-solving.

Hobbies

Our brains thrive on variety. A newborn infant arrives with his receptors wide open, responding to stimuli. This process continues throughout life (if we allow it). People who perform mostly mental tasks—including most of us as "knowledge workers"—profit most from hobbies that are physical in nature, activities in which we move our hands and feet.

Avocations involving building and constructing tend to be more stimulating than collecting-type interests. Gardening, railroad modeling, sewing, and woodworking illustrate the change of pace one needs. Ancient Hebrew rabbis were compelled to learn a trade not only for enrichment and expansion of their minds and experience but also for self-support in time of persecution.

Our discretionary time should be filled with choices of constructive activities that provide a contrast to what we do most of the time. The shifting of mental gears appears to kindle new thought patterns and thereby make our lives more fulfilling.

Fine Arts

It is no accident that many creative people may be classified as "artsy." Music, drama, painting, and a variety of other skills provide a kind of atomic fission of emotional energy to enhance generativity.

In his helpful book *What to Listen for in Music,* the well-known composer Aaron Copland identified four elements: rhythm, melody, harmony, and tone color. Then he distinguished three kinds of musical textures.[1] Because he is the quintessential artist in a democratic society, he explained that listening to music as a free but informed spirit touches the deepest part of our beings and enriches our lives.

"When Mozart was 14 years old, he listened to a secret mass in Rome, Allegri's *Miserere*. The composition had been guarded as a mystery; the singers were not allowed to transcribe it on pain of excommunication. Mozart heard it only once. He was then able to reproduce the entire score.

"Let no one think that this was exclusively a feat of prodigious memory. The mass was a piece of art and, as such, had threads of simplicity. The structure is the essence of the art. The child who was to become one of the world's greatest composers may not have been able to remember the details of this complicated work, but he could identify the threads, remember them, and reinvent the details having listened once with consummate attention."

—*Author Unknown*

Reading

Print is the natural habitat of ideas. A book can give a life-giving transplant, without anesthesia. I mentioned reading earlier, but we need to understand that "to read without reflecting is like eating without digesting," according to Edmund Burke. Readers tend to be leaders—*if* their reading is active, not passive. That is, one needs to read mind-stretching material, not something that merely fortifies prejudices.

Reading is to the mind what exercise is to the body. Creativity thrives on wide and wise reading.

It's not necessary to have the highest I.Q. to be a creative person, but it's hard be creative without becoming an omnivorous reader. Read (or skim) books on a regular basis, week by week. Keep a tape recorder or 3" x 5" cards handy to record ideas as they occur. Sometimes it is better to skim than to read in depth. For that, consider articles, digests, or condensed books on tape. Above all, understand that the reading and study of the Bible is a postgraduate course in the richest library of human experience.

Research demonstrates that people who do not use their brains will lose some of their mental capability as they grow older. By perpetually engaging one's mind through reading, innovative people can help sustain their mental capacity. Embrace the motto "Use it or lose it!"

And don't forget the alternative to reading, which is listening. I'm an avid listener to books on tape while driving in my car, because it has opened up vast opportunities for mind improvement. Similarly, learning a language, taking training in a skill, gaining motivation, or examining biblical insights can all be done while engaged in something else, thanks to the invention of the simple audiocassette.

I don't know about you, but every time I walk into a bookstore and see all that is available to us today, I ask myself, "How can I find the time to read so many worthwhile books?"

Writing

Francis Bacon commented that reading makes a full man, writing an exact man. While reading requires receptivity, writing demands reaching into a deep pocket of creative craftsmanship.

Not everyone approaches the art of writing with ease and comfort. But those who labor to develop their artistry with words experience a profound satisfaction—that of fashioning into language ideas clothed in a wardrobe fit for the occasion. Like a well-groomed speaker ascending the podium, the right words dress thoughts for eager consumption. The Roman statesman Cicero (106–43 B. C.) put it this way: "The aim of writing is not simply to be understood, but to make it impossible to be misunderstood."

The truly creative writer becomes rarer in our world of sound bytes and visually oriented media. We live in an age of inflated words that have little real currency. Therefore our writing must combine both style and substance.

G. K. Chesterton thoughtfully observed, "The *Iliad* is great because all of life is a battle; the *Odyssey* is great because all of life is a journey; the book of Job is great because all of life is a riddle."

I concur. We need Christian writing that resonates with reality. Consider that the Holy Spirit Himself used the scroll and the printing press for the most creative message ever proclaimed. Paul Harvey once wrote that there is no scalpel ever honed as sharp as a ballpoint pen. "With that lethal instrument," he wrote, "you can destroy a man, subvert a government."[2] (I would add that you can also teach, console, and amuse.)

A former executive director of the Academy of Christian Editors reminds us that the practical discipline of writing is easily measured, but what is not so easily gauged is the interior discipline of being open to new ideas. Here is the focus of the creative mind—freshness, aliveness!

In time, you may feel prompted to write an article for a magazine or a church paper, and with more experience, even a book. Writing letters affords a good way to practice the art. But write whenever possible. Even a page or two a day could lead to a book in a year. It is not beyond most of us; the key is rewriting and objective evaluation.

English critic Cyril Connolly suggested, "Better to write for yourself and have no public, than to write for the public and have no self." When you write, you give your readers a chance to look into the inner workings of your mind and heart. The act of putting thoughts on a page forces you to evaluate your ideas more objectively than when you merely think about them. For that reason, creative writing is the sweetest agony known to man. Socrates liked to refer to himself as a "literary midwife," someone who helped ideas to birth out of a laboring mind, a "master of cerebral obstetrics."

Asking Questions

As Roy Zuck noted, "There is a skill in asking questions that arouse curiosity, stimulate interest, challenge thinking, guide student learning, and correct false assumptions."[3]

The systematic use of questions stems from overwhelming curiosity and healthy skepticism. That is why children tend to learn so rapidly; they never stop asking questions. If you want to regain that sense of childlike wonder and curiosity, I encourage you to ask "What if" questions. Also observe what others do and then ask yourself, "What would I do?" The uncreative mind may easily spot wrong answers, but it takes a creative mind to spot wrong questions. Also make sure your mind is not so full of questions that there is no room for answers.

My father taught me, "Son, when you are in the presence of significant people who know more than you do, keep your mouth shut except to ask penetrating questions." That advice has proven to be a lifelong treasure. I've discovered one learns more by listening than by talking.

"If I had thought about it, I wouldn't have done the experiment. The literature was full of examples that said you can't do this."

—Spencer Silver, commenting on how he developed the adhesive for 3-M's Post-It notes.

Recently when I flew from Dallas to New York City I was seated beside an advertising executive. He was like a dam of words waiting to burst. All I did to launch the conversation was to ask, "Tell me what kind of work you do." As he spoke, I asked a few follow-up why-and-how queries. I got a mini-education on the subject of the modern advertising industry. When we landed in the Big Apple, he commented, "You know, this has been one of the most fascinating conversations I've ever had." I agreed. I had said little but learned much.

Questions are the badge of a good teacher. Anyone who thinks he has all the answers is not up to date on the questions. G. Campbell Morgan perceptively commented, "Faith is the answer to a question; and, therefore, it is out of work when there is no question to ask."

Idea-Spurring Questions

- Put to other uses? New ways to use as is? Other uses if modified?
- Adapt? What else is like this? What other ideas does this suggest?
- Modify? Change meaning, color, motion, sound, order, taste, form, shape?
- Magnify? What to add? Greater frequency? Stronger? Larger? Plus ingredient? Multiply?
- Minify? What to subtract? Divide? Eliminate? Smaller? Lighter? Slower? Split up? Less frequency?
- Substitute? Who else instead? What else instead? Other place? Other time?
- Rearrange? Other layout? Other sequence? Change Pace?
- Reverse? Opposites? Turn it backwards? Turn it upside down? Turn it inside out?
- Combine? A blend? An assortment? Combine purposes? Combine ideas?

Spend Time with Creative People

With some people you spend an evening; with creative people you invest it.

Remember that everyone is an authority on his or her own experiences. So listen carefully when you have the privilege of spending time with others, especially individuals with expertise. That's why I like physicians; their knowledge of how the body works fascinates me. I'm sure the same could be said for other professionals. Sometimes these folks can upset your preconceived notions. You may disagree, but you will be stretched and stimulated.

If you really want to tap the riches of other people's wisdom and experience, consider putting together your own "think tank" of people with various backgrounds and perspectives who meet periodically to discuss ideas, problems, books, and the like. Never forget that none of us is as smart as all of us, as Steve Jobs used to say. And the wisest of all men wrote, "As iron sharpens iron, so one person sharpens another" (Prov. 17:17).

I'm not suggesting that you try to activate all the suggestions in this chapter at once. You'll only get frustrated. But do begin with one or two. Then, as time goes by you'll be able to add others.

The point is that if you continue to be exposed to the same things without change, you will atrophy and become stagnant as a person. This shriveling is not an option for the committed Christian. Paul wrote that each believer is a "new creation" in Christ (2 Cor. 5:17). The Savior grew (Luke 2:52) and so must we. Christ's life in us stirs a desire to be creative, and we need to be proactive in seeking daily to reflect His unlimited gifts through how we learn and live.

Exercises

1.   Here's an inventory based on the activities mentioned in this chapter. Evaluate yourself to see which ones you are actively engaged in already, and which ones you could consider cultivating.

	Nonexistent			Highly Developed	
Experience	1	2	3	4	5
Problem-solving	1	2	3	4	5
Hobbies	1	2	3	4	5

Fine arts	1	2	3	4	5
Reading	1	2	3	4	5
Writing	1	2	3	4	5
Questions	1	2	3	4	5
People	1	2	3	4	5

What specifically can you do to improve in each area? Set some realistic goals that compel you to step up the stairs rather than to stare up the steps.

2. Within the lifetime of most people reading this book, most hardware stores had a testing board for testing television vacuum tubes, and they stocked an array of replacement tubes. Today, the vacuum-tube industry is essentially nonexistent. The same could be said for other industries. Suppose there was no longer a need for the job you currently do. Think up three scenarios for how you would provide for yourself. (One of them cannot be welfare!)

3. In the first chapter I mentioned that every three years Peter Drucker begins a study of some new area he has never before investigated. Identify one new area you would like to learn about during the next year, something you have never before studied in depth. What practical strategies can you think of for learning about this area?

Helpful Resource

- Johnson, Ken C., and John H. Coe. *Wildlife in the Kingdom Come.* Grand Rapids: Zondervan, 1993.

Creative Problem-Solving

Problems are like weeds; the more you ignore them the faster they grow.

—ANCIENT PROVERB

8

When Adam and Eve stepped out of their privileged roles in the Garden of Eden and defaulted on their stewardship assignment, they forfeited their perfect habitat. But more significantly, they created a problem of cosmic proportions. All of God's perfect creation was doomed. His children were in disgrace, on death row, and His plan for the earth appeared to be totally ruined.

Any problem we have, no matter how overwhelming, could never approach the enormity of what God faced after His human creatures willfully disobeyed Him. It is imperative, therefore, that we who are part of that Fall look closely at the solutions the Almighty Creator put into action in order to salvage the destruction that lay at His feet.

We ought never to minimize or underestimate the nature of the problems that confront us. On the other hand, we ought never to minimize or underestimate our ability to solve them.

Indeed, sometimes we can't afford not to solve them. A professor in a college ethics class presented his students with a problem. He said, "A man has syphilis and his wife has tuberculosis. They have had four children; one has died, the other three have what is considered a terminal illness. The mother is pregnant. What do you recommend?" After a spirited discussion the majority of the class voted that she abort the child. "Fine," said the professor, "you have just killed Beethoven."[1]

God has written down for us what to do in the face of failure and its twin, discouragement, amid the seemingly irreversible trend toward banal weariness in our world. God never created an entity—whether an individual, a marriage, or a group—that was doomed to failure. All His enterprises are destined for some form of prosperity, invested with His power and fully funded with His riches. From the Creator Himself, look at the biblical disentanglements, the rules for repair of damage. These principles apply to individuals, to groups in our Christian churches and organizations, to any bracket of people where things have gone wrong.

Remember that creative behavior marked by captivating, delightful surprises does not arise from problem-imprisoned people. We must master the art of finding solutions based on biblical principles and know that ultimately there are no insolubles.

Biblical Creativity Commits to Change

The Christian life is a life of transformation, a shift of attitudes, values, thinking, and behavior. Allow yourself to be stunned as you contemplate Romans 8:29, which says that we as believers are predestined to be conformed to the image of Jesus Christ. If that is the case, cataclysmic changes must take place! Romans 12:2 commands us to be transformed ("metamorphosized"), and 2 Corinthians 3:18 spells out the process: transformed into His likeness with ever-increasing glory, which comes from the Lord, who is the Spirit.

Our model is found in the New Testament. The early church was not a perfect body of believers, but it was a progressing one, striving to obey the principles taught by Christ and His disciples. Wherever there are people, there are problems. To live is to have problems; to solve problems is to grow personally and spiritually.

I saw a church sign that read, "New Testament Church." *Which one?* I wondered. The carnal church at Corinth? The church at Ephesus, which left her first love? The church at Sardis, with its reputation that lacked reality? Or the one at Laodicea, which was nauseating, despite its affluence? These were groups externally prosperous but internally indigent.

There are no perfect churches, for there are no perfect people—*yet*. Eventually there will be, but for now, people must change. For one thing, they must change as they live in a fast-changing society. Change is the tissue of life. Problems are only opportunities clad in blue jeans.

Change Always Involves Problem-Solving

Human beings are problem-solvers by nature, yet many of us have come to think that happiness is the absence of problems. It's not. The total absence of problems is the beginning of death—for individuals and institutions.

James 1:2–12 details the problem-solving process in the life of a Christian. Problems are God's chisel to shape the soul. He tests us to develop us, and He urges us not to give up or perform an abortion on His divine purposes. Testing sculpts us to more closely resemble Jesus Christ. We all want the product of Christlikeness, but we shun the process.

Everything that comes into the believer's life scrolls across the screen of God's will. To agree with that statement is to affirm the sovereignty of our God. He is altogether loving and merciful, graciously allowing what is eminently good and best for us. Problems are all a part of His custom-designed curriculum. Therefore we should ask God "What?" but never "Why?" What is God teaching me through this experience? Many of us, however, fail to address that question adequately. We need to look at our model Problem-Solver, the Holy Spirit. We'll see that learning must build its foundation on four fundamental, indispensable issues.

Address the Root Problem at Hand

Reaching a decision without really deciding has become a modern art form. Today we conduct public opinion polls and let the polls settle our decisions. We employ the Kinsey method of statistical morality: If enough people do it, it's all right. Even we in the church are guilty of this approach. We look at what other highly visible, large, and successful churches are doing and assume their approach must be right for our church too.

Not true! We have a dire need to address root problems, not surface issues. Failure to do so can lead to disaster. A 1904 fire aboard the "unsinkable" *General Slocum*, a Royal Mail river steamer, illustrates vividly the necessity of finding out what is really wrong.

The paddlewheeler left Third Street pier on Manhattan's Lower East Side bound for North Brother Island near the Bronx. Working-class people—1,358 of them—were aboard for a gala church outing. Approximately a half hour before the scheduled docking, a fire broke out. Even though the boat was close to shore and people were shouting, urging it to land, the captain kept his course steady into the wind. No one knows why he did not alter his course toward the land or stop at another small island where help was available.

Some think the captain did not appreciate the gravity of the situation; others hold that he believed the crew could contain the fire. Whatever the reason, this disaster, possibly the worst inland accident in United States history, cost more than one thousand lives. Later investigation discovered that the crew was unskilled and untrained and that inspectors had been bribed. Fire buckets had been stuffed with garbage; life vests were filled with rotted cork, and even the lifeboats had been tethered with bailing wire.[2]

The excerpt, "Could Creativity Have Helped on the Titanic" (facing page), is designed to help you utilize your creativity.

The estrangement of our first parents, whatever their rationale, left God "holding the bag," so to speak. What did He do? He addressed the problem. Note that He did not turn His back; instead, He initiated reconciliation, searching for His children. Then He spoke to them honestly, spelling out the consequences for their actions. But His father's heart announced that the harsh realism of the debacle did not prevent His loving them back to life and fruitfulness.

Through His spokesmen, God clearly defined the problem and wrote it down to remind all succeeding generations: "Your iniquities have separated you from your God . . . hidden his face from you" (Isa. 59:2). "All have sinned and fallen short of the glory of God" (Rom. 3:23). "If we claim to be without sin, we deceive ourselves and the truth is not in us" (1 John 1:8).

Too many people in our Christian communities are staking their spiritual welfare on leaders who keep sailing along, hoping that things will get better. There is no substitute for reality checks, for confronting sin.

Could Creativity Have Helped on the *Titanic?*

In the early morning of April 15, 1912, the British ship *Titanic* struck an iceberg and sank in less than two hours. More than 1,500 passengers perished. An investigation found that there were not nearly enough lifeboats onboard. Moreover, many of the lifeboats sent away from the sinking ship were only partially filled.

Without diminishing the utter tragedy of this needless disaster, the sinking of the *Titanic* raises an interesting issue of creativity. A common mistake in solving problems is a commitment to only one solution, thereby eliminating other possibilities. Could it be that a contributing factor to the loss of life on the *Titanic* was an overcommitment to one solution—the lifeboats?

Try this exercise with a small group. Imagine that you are passengers on the *Titanic.* All the lifeboats have pulled away, filled mainly with women and children. Thus you are left on the doomed ship. Is your fate sealed? You have perhaps an hour or more of time. At your disposal is the largest and most lavishly appointed ship the world has seen to date. You have 1,500 people to work with, mostly men. How many solutions can you devise to save at least some of your lives?

Don't panic—use your creativity!

Reestablish the Supply Lines

Wilted, worn-out people and ministries invariably wither because of a lack of nourishment. People need love, encouragement, training, clarification, and support—food for their spiritual souls.

Before I was married, I visited a country church with my future wife's family, a small group of believers with all the signs of a lingering terminal illness. That the church was small—probably less than one hundred members—was not the problem. After all, it was located in a small town. No, the underlying malady was spiritual starvation. Its teaching was empty.

Then along came an unsophisticated preacher who adopted a circuit of three churches in the area. He was far from flashy, but he preached and taught a creative message straight from the Word of God. Almost immediately, the church began to grow. A youth group was formed, and he discipled the people to explore new areas of outreach. Their basic resources were restored.

Mend the Weather-Beaten Fences

With the onset of stunted growth and decay in human experience, there comes inevitably an erosion of relationships. The little country church I mentioned was riddled with petty quarrels, jealousies, and controversies. Family and community connections were badly in need of recovery. Forgiveness cried out to be heard.

Paul addressed this very issue in Philippians, his mental-health manual. Two women in that assembly were at odds with each other, women who had formerly teamed up with Paul in his ministry there. To them he simply urged an end to it all. Then he shared a five-part recipe for conflict resolution: (1) "Rejoice in the Lord," that is, get beyond yourselves and look to the Lord. (2) "Let your gentleness be evident to all." In other words speak with kindness to each other. (3) "Do not be anxious." Relax, and give it all to God. (4) "Be thankful." The simple act of expressing gratitude for our blessings takes the heat out of infection. (5) Present your requests to God. Prayer realigns us and restores peace (Phil. 4:1–7).

Return to Your Assigned Task

David clearly explained that God has no unassigned places in His human family (Ps. 139). Each of us in His royal household has received spiritual gifts and an inheritance of untold resources. We are responsible to develop them and invest accordingly.

I think of an urban church where a hurtful disagreement has resulted in division and the loss of a sizable number of its members. Many of these people are mature believers. They have been realistic and forgiving. But the final repair work, getting back to full productivity, has never really occurred. The original group still limps along, lacking the vitality that should accompany the healing process. They have not allowed testing to "finish its work so that [they] may be mature" (James 1:4).

Problems Potentiate Progress

Hebrews 5:8 informs us that even the Lord was not exempt from suffering. In verse 14 the writer defined spiritual maturity for us as the ability to distinguish good from evil. When the Scriptures are constantly used by the believer, he enrolls in a self-training program with guaranteed results. There can be no genuine growth apart from problem-solving. It is a learned skill.

Proverbs 14:4 introduces us to the reality of life: "Where no oxen are, the trough is clean; but much increase comes by the strength of an ox" (NKJV). You want no problems? Never put an ox in the stall. No mess, no ministry!

Warren Bennis, distinguished professor of business administration at the University of Southern California, perceptively observed, "Most of us have experienced the terrible frustration of being part of a group that had the potential for greatness, but never quite jelled. The geometrical surge in ideas and energy that happens in Great Groups never took place, even though the talent was there, the drive was there, and the project seemed full of promise. Looking back at these stillborn opportunities, you experience a shudder of sadness and inevitably ask yourself, 'What went wrong?'"[3]

The question is not whether we will face problems requiring solutions but whether we have a realistic approach to solving them. Problems may be as simple as what to do on a vacation or which shirt to wear. Or the inquiry may embrace a much more serious matter, such as whom to marry, how to care for homeless people in our community, or how to plant a church.

In our society of rapid and pervasive change, problems surround us like the air we breathe. Can we devise a practical and workable template for confronting them? Creative problem-solving is a structured way of attacking a problem, beginning with a mess and ending with an action plan.

Consider what happens when you attempt to put together a jigsaw puzzle. First, you might look for border pieces, then pieces of the same color. You also keep the picture on the front of the box in front of you, so you can match up the interlocking snippets of the puzzle. Using strategies like these, you not only complete the puzzle; you also learn the *process* for solving jigsaw puzzles. So it is with seeking to find answers to your creative problems.

Groups are often minimally effective because they have no pattern for solving problems. I propose a five-stage template, each stage combining divergent thinking (to generate as many suggestions as possible) and convergent thinking (which selects the best ideas for further development). Within each step the group uses a variety of creative techniques to challenge people to think deeply and differently about a given dilemma.

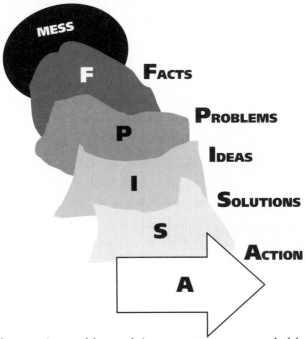

The creative problem-solving process recommended has five parts. The following is an overview, with definitions of each stage:

1. *Fact-finding stage,* which includes the gathering and analyzing of data in preparation for defining the problem.
2. *Problem-finding stage,* which analyzes the many unmanageable areas in order to point up the central problem to be solved.
3. *Idea-finding stage,* which embraces idea generation, processing, and development of numerous possible leads to the solution.
4. *Solution-finding stage,* which evaluates potential solutions against defined criteria.

5. *Action-finding stage*, which involves the development and adoption of a plan of action, plus the implementation of the chosen solution.

Now let's look at the specifics:

Fact-Finding

All problem-solving begins with a mess, that is, an ill-defined challenge. Messes are discovered in several ways: Someone or a group of people is hurting; persistent complaints constantly surface, perhaps in a survey; a deviation from scriptural norms is detected; things are going wrong; or there is a desire to improve. Problem-sensitivity picks up the confusion, often as a result of evaluation and feedback.

Problem-Solving	Problem	Opportunity Searching/Seeing
Where we are _____		Where do we want to be?
	Gap	

In this stage we need a realistic and comprehensive data stream. The more input we can secure, the greater the potential for solution. We tend to look *at* facts rather than *for* them. New facts invariably trigger new ideas. Observation always makes us more sensitive, not only to the problems, but also to the possibilities and challenges involved. Therefore bombard the problem with questions, because they are the creative acts of a well-disciplined mind.

Of J. R. Cominsky, noted publisher of the *Saturday Review* (1942–68), someone has commented, "Given a problem with nine parts marked 'impossible' and one part 'possible,' he had no difficulty in inverting the equation and making it work." Cominsky serves as a useful model for us. The problems of church or society cannot be solved by skeptics or cynics whose horizons are limited by unrealism or unbelief. We need people willing to change the equation from "No way" to "I'll find a way." In time, people like that hear, "Way to go!"

Problem-Finding

Suppose I visit my physician with a splitting headache. He'll ask me a host of probing questions. "Look, Doc," I'll say, "all I want is to get rid of my headache." "Well, then, let me write a prescription and you'll never have another headache."

Two weeks later, I'm dead. Has he solved my problem? Permanently! But no good physician treats only symptoms. He addresses the underlying disease. In his examination he may discover that I have a brain tumor, but in treating the real problem, my headache, backache, and all other subproblems disappear.

This difficult process of diagnosing root problems often leads to fuzzy thinking. Something is wrong, but you don't know precisely what. A definition of the problem is required, and you must search for it. Many issues are tied up with subproblems. Like a careful diagnostician, you must not stop with attacking symptoms.

If the core problem is cured, the symptoms will disappear. If you solve only a subproblem, a symptom, you may continue to be plagued with the real disease—which may be terminal.

Recall the wise words of Charles Kettering, engineer-inventor: "A problem well defined is a problem half solved." Take time to describe the problem as presented. Time is never wasted in pinpointing the underlying issue, the basic difficulty. All too often we concentrate on the quick fix, taking pride in coming up with solutions immediately after discovering the problem. But research continues to support the thesis that the time taken to plan at the front end is inversely proportional to the time required for execution of the solution.

The new formulation of a problem is often far more essential than the solution. For optimum idea stimulation, refine your statement of the problem.

For example, a parishioner tells you, "The problem, Pastor, is that my wife annoys me." By stating the problem that way, this man has severely narrowed his range of ideas. How much better to ask, "How can my wife and I learn to get along better?"

This need to reframe our problems is a common, everyday experience. Have you ever complained, "There just isn't enough time to do everything"? This way of stating things blames time, which is not likely to cooperate in improving the dilemma. A better approach is to ask, "In what ways can I rearrange my priorities to give me more time?" Now we're making progress!

There are three crippling tendencies in forming a problem-statement: overgeneralization, blaming someone else, and inadequate data. All three fail to address root causes. For example, take the statement, "Church attendance is declining." This hand-wringing lament simply gives information, but it doesn't probe for causes. It focuses on the problem, not the cause. What are the reasons attendance is down?

The following diagram describes the creative problem-solving process to this point.

IDENTIFYING THE PROBLEM

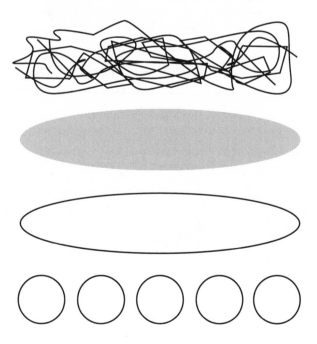

Idea-Finding

The French philosopher Emile Chartier warned, "Nothing is more dangerous than an idea when it is the only one you have." Therefore list every conceivable idea you can as to how the problem might be solved. Be sure to defer judgment while doing this. Then, after you or your group have mentally exhausted yourselves listing alternatives, go back and apply judgment in selecting the one(s) you feel have the most potential.

The caption for a cartoon featuring a pastor conferring with a group of subordinates reads, "I want your fresh and honest ideas; don't hold back, even if it costs you your job." Unfortunately this is sometimes true, but lethal!

The idea-finding stage makes use of the most creative tools for generating a plethora of ideas; for example, brainstorming, plussing, objection-countering, five-sensing, gaming, and other strategies that we'll consider later. Getting one step closer to a final solution involves a combination of individual and group ideation. Strengthen the individuals, and you strengthen the group.

Two of the top needs in the church today are analyzing the process of group behavior and teaching people how to use group process. Unfortunately most of us are trained to function as individuals but then expected to function as part of a team. Nowhere does the role of Body Life become more critical than in problem-solving. We must utilize all the gifts in the body of Christ, and first they must be discovered.

Nowhere is prayer more essential than in the problem-solving process. Listen to Eugene Peterson's trenchant analysis: "Civilization is littered with unsolved problems, baffling impasses. The best minds of the world are at the end of their tether. The most knowledgeable observers of our condition are badly frightened. The most relevant contribution that Christians make at these points of impasse is the act of prayer—determined, repeated, leisurely meetings with a personal and living God. New life is conceived in these meetings."[4]

You can always do more after you have prayed, but you cannot do more until you have prayed. Prayer needs to permeate the decision-making process.

Solution-Finding

PROBLEM   **IDEAS**   **ALTERNATE SOLUTIONS**

Now the group needs to surface criteria by which to evaluate ideas and alternative solutions. Recall Abraham Maslow's aphorism, "If the only tool you have is a hammer, all problems look like nails." Think, for example, about the selection of a piece of property for possible purchase by your church. When faced with a decision involving solutions that provide different outcomes, consider the use of the decision-making matrix below:

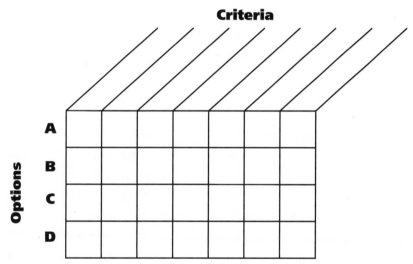

Action-Finding

This level of problem-solving demands a plan of action. Lack of such a plan dooms most decision-making to failure. The group may have an excellent discussion and come up with practical suggestions, but there are no decisions and no action points.

These questions need to be answered and put into the minutes for every decision:

- What did we decide?
- Who is responsible?
- When will it be completed?
- What budgetary provisions have been made?

"In preparing for battle, I have always found that plans are useless, but planning is indispensable."

—*General Dwight D. Eisenhower*

Six keys open the window of acceptance.

1. *Communication.* This is a sales task. How do we get others to buy into our decision when they have not been through our process? This is a problem of perception. Avoid assuming that others see it as you do. Ask these three helpful questions:
   - How can we provide reasons and information to gain acceptance?
   - What are the advantages of our plan *for them?*
   - How can we dramatize the advantages to make them more obvious?

2. *Anticipation.* The process of anticipatory thinking is essential. What will be the objections? How can these be forestalled and overcome? What will be the impact? What if . . . ?

A member of a local church in Texas was asked to plan the annual picnic. He did a splendid job except for one serious omission. I asked him, "What are your plans if it rains?" "Hendricks," he smiled confidently, "It doesn't rain in Texas in August." I countered, "What if it does?" He had no plan. You guessed it! In very uncharacteristic fashion, it poured on the day of the picnic. Guess whose face was red and whose picnic plans washed out.

3. *Assistance.* What individuals or groups can we get to cooperate with us in implementing this plan?

4. *Location.* What is the best venue for putting this plan into action?

5. *Timing.* What is the best time to launch this idea? Considering the people involved, would there be a better time? Check the calendar. What regular occasion might be used to launch this program? How can we prepare?

6. *Precautions.* Whenever possible, pre-test any idea. Ask, What can be done to ensure its effectiveness? Have you talked to other people, other groups who may have used this plan? What did

they learn from their experience? Do you have a checklist for unforeseen problems (extra light bulbs, extension cords, childcare, props, etc.)? Can you limit the possibilities of initial failure?

In the action/implementation phase, you need two components.

1. *A feedback loop.* Be sure to ask the right people. For example, ask mothers about the children's programs. Ask the teenagers regarding the youth ministry. You are seeking reliable, objective data from the people directly involved.

2. *Internal and external evaluation.* Ask questions like: How do we think we did? How do others perceive our performance? It is sometimes possible that everyone overlooked an obvious possibility. Recall the illustration of the church property purchase. Did anyone ask about future expansion plans? Has anyone checked with the city planning commission for this neighborhood?

The greatest miscalculation in IBM history occurred in 1957 when that company assumed only fifty-two computers would be sold worldwide! The thinking you do now will determine both the quality and impact of your people in the next generation. This critical measurement must be an ongoing process, and it always leads to improvement.

Pierce J. Howard provides a usable tool to help discern the kinds of problem-solving activity demanded for different kinds of problems.[5]

Kinds of Problems and the Nature of Their Solution

Kind of Problem	*Nature of Appropriate Problem-Solving Activity*
Problem with unknown cause	Finding the cause
Problem with known cause or cause irrelevant	Generating ideas that could fix the problem
Decision among solutions with certain outcomes	Deciding on the best solution
Decision among solutions with uncertain outcomes	Deciding which solution has high probability of success
A jumbled list	Determining priority order

Caution Signs

Problem-solving is usually a complex and time-consuming procedure. H. L. Mencken shrewdly observed, "There is always an easy solution to every human problem—neat, plausible, and wrong." If we do not carefully bathe our plans in prayer, this negative description is tailor-made for our Christian community and our nation. We Americans have a proclivity for shortcuts and easy answers. In seeking to fit into our culture, we are in chronic danger.

William Willimon, dean of the Duke University chapel, warns us, "In leaning over to speak to the modern world, I fear we may have fallen in. While we are attempting to build a bridge it appears the traffic is moving in only one direction." Albert Einstein adds a provocative thought: "You cannot solve a problem on the same level it was created. You have to rise above it to the next level." How applicable to the Christian life! Jesus reminded His disciples, "Apart from me you can do nothing" (John 15:5). When we look at thorny issues from Christ's perspective, the right solutions begin to emerge.

Ideas and solutions always depend on the aim and expectation of a person or group. Like a built-in compass, this pre-set thinking direction ultimately skews the outcome.

Our task is not to speak to the culture but to change it!

Exercises

1. Identify one nagging problem you would like to solve. Then work through the five-stage process outlined in the chapter:
    *   *Fact-finding.* What are the facts that indicate this problem really is a problem? Is there pain? Are there complaints? Is there sin? Are things going wrong? Is there a desire to improve?
    *   *Problem-finding.* What are the symptoms of this problem, and what is the root of the problem? Be careful you don't come to conclusions too quickly! How can you determine what is the real, underlying core of the problem?
    *   *Idea-finding.* What ideas can you generate for dealing with this problem? (See chapter 9 on Brainstorming.)

106

- *Solution-finding.* How will you know when the problem is solved? Which one of the ideas you came up with earlier addresses the root problem? Which ideas seem the most likely to solve the problem? Which ideas seem realistic? Is it possible that solving the problem may require a combination of ideas or solutions?
- *Action-finding.* What steps have to be taken to implement the solution(s) you have chosen for the problem? What will the solution require in time and schedule, effort, money, and logistics? To implement your solution(s), with whom do you need to communicate?

2. Try going through the process outlined above with a group.
3. The Nine Dots Exercise
   Without lifting your pencil from the paper, draw four straight, connected lines so that they go through each of the nine dots only once. After you have tried a couple different ways, ask yourself what restrictions you have set up in your mind in solving this problem.

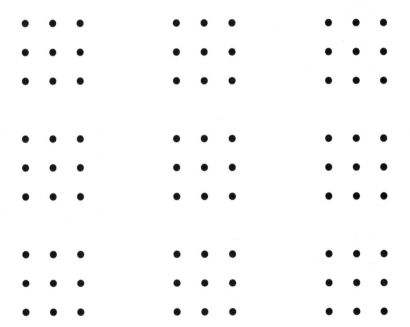

(Answers can be found on page 242)

Helpful Resource

- *The Encyclopedia of Ice Breakers.* San Francisco: Jossey-Bass, 1983.

Brainstorming

The best way to have a good idea is to have lots of ideas.

—LINUS PAULING

9

Henry Ford once called in an efficiency expert to examine his company. He received a favorable report, with one exception. "One employee down the corridor just sits there with his feet on his desk. He's wasting your money," the specialist reported.

"That man," replied Ford, "once had an idea that saved us millions of dollars. At the time, I believe his feet were planted right where they are now."

The search for good ideas is a never-ending treasure hunt, scavenging the minds of men and women for the tailor-made solution to the matter at hand. It is a universal pursuit, often disappointing, always a rigorous and meticulous investigation.

Like a competent athlete the human brain excels in mental calisthenics. From the time we are born, we use an endless variety of thinking procedures; and as we have seen already, more kinds of thinking produce more creative behavior. Nine widely used techniques can help you master innovative productions.

- Brainstorming
- Plussing
- Five-sensing

- Objection-countering
- Gaming
- Mind-mapping
- Roles
- Thinking hats
- Storyboarding

I want to highlight and recommend these strategies as possible means to meeting personal and ministry needs for the coming generations.

The Origin and Definition of Brainstorming

Let's begin with brainstorming. No technique has been more widely employed in business organizations and advertising agencies than brainstorming. Only the church has been reluctant, and our cultural lag is costly. The purpose of brainstorming is to generate a maximum number of new ideas and to record every suggestion verbatim. A planning group should use this technique early in the process.

The history of this art dates back to the Creative Problem-Solving focus at the University of Buffalo. Alex Osborne's landmark book, *Applied Imagination*, was the first to publicize the technique.[1] Since then, the Disney Corporation has made the most extensive use of it in designing and developing Disneyland and Disney World, as well as films and other products.

A definition of the process describes what many people have done sporadically but without a concentrated effort. Everyone thinks he has an answer to a given problem; brainstorming allows all suggestions to come forth. It is a rapid and free association in which judgment is suspended. The process is designed to jump-start the brain and is used most profitably to generate new ideas and solve problems. A versatile technique, it can be used individually or in groups.

Brainstorming Rules

The rules for brainstorming groom this technique, preventing stereotypical thinking and getting out of old ruts.

Absolutely No Criticism Is Allowed

Criticism is the mortician of the creative process. We develop a tendency to hesitate and evaluate an idea before stating it. Ideally we are looking for a freeflow of suggestions, unfettered by judgmental thinking. To get that, we must keep the environment positive. If not, few ideas are generated, and potentially good ones will be lost. The principle is to think first and judge later. Jettison your uneducated conscience.

I recommend that the leader employ a bell to ring every time a negative criticism is proffered. That adds a light touch to the process, but it also produces a sensitivity to the tendency to condemn.

The More Ideas the Better

There is a direct correlation between the number of ideas generated and the number of usable ideas. Embrace the principle that quantity is the shortest possible distance to quality. Practice, as in any skill, improves both the process and the product.

It is helpful to remember that only 6 percent of one's ideas are usually any good. So how many ideas must you generate to get one good idea? And how many good ones must you generate to get a great one? The conclusion is obvious: The more the better.

The Wilder the Better

You can always tame an idea, but you cannot pump one up. Wild ideas indicate creative thinking. Risk-taking pervades the process. Uninhibited thinking leads to unique solutions. This involves approaching a problem or a subject from a fresh perspective. Far-fetched speculations are accepted because they often trigger more practical ideas.

Hitchhiking Is Permitted, Even Encouraged

What one person says, regardless of its individual value, may stimulate someone else's thinking or remind another of a different or better insight. An original idea may be weak and unusable, but an additional suggestion strengthens it. It is a process of piggybacking, building on or expanding ideas expressed by others. People tend to potentiate each other.

The Value of Brainstorming

Brainstorming Generates Ideas

Using brainstorming, an individual or group can produce vastly more ideas in sixty seconds than would have occurred in a traditional setting. The assignment to brainstorm places a burr under people's mental saddles. A good session should be lively and enthusiastic; no one thinks about whether an idea is good or bad. Instead, the free-wheeling character of newness creates spontaneity.

I remember a group of Sunday-school teachers who thought they could not teach a certain lesson without using flannelgraph. (They were *very* traditional.) But by agreeing to brainstorm together, they came up with seventy alternatives within five minutes!

> **"Salsa companies are introducing products at the rate of three hundred per year."**
>
> —Fast Company

Brainstorming Changes Attitudes

People become more open to new ideas and develop a profound respect and appreciation for their own deep well of knowledge.

Brainstorming Develops Confidence

This is true of both individuals and groups. The synergy ignited demonstrates that latent thinking can grow exponentially.

Brainstorming Builds Teamwork

In the context of ministry, a new appreciation for the body of Christ often results from the brainstorming process. The best groups draw together different kinds of people, who may not even be close friends. But when working together for a common goal, they soon bond together, proving Steve Jobs's adage, "None of us is as smart as all of us."

Suggestions

Brainstorming can be greatly facilitated if the following ideas are implemented.

Teach the Brainstorming Process

Introduce the process at a leader's retreat. This will equip and provide experience for them to use the same techniques with their people. It will also strengthen the group as they see another way to work together.

Begin with a Fun Assignment

This approach is like an aerobic exercise before the real game. Don't start off with the heavy lifting. Give folks a chance to warm up. (Some of their mental muscles may be badly out of shape!)

Try this: Place a common object—such as a brick, a coin, a paper clip, or a straw—before the group and ask how many different ways it could be used other than for its traditional purpose. As the group gets into it, suddenly a lighthearted spirit will develop, releasing tension. This nonthreatening warm-up gets the group ready for more serious contemplation.

Be sure to vary the pace of the meeting to accommodate different thinking styles, and follow brainstorming with more contemplative techniques.

Employ an Administrative Assistant

You'll need a secretary to record on a legal pad, whiteboard, or newsprint all the ideas that are generated. The size of the group will determine how much is produced. Ideally six to eight persons can be very productive. If you have more, break the group into smaller units. If there are too many people, a group tends to develop spectators or a lunatic fringe; too few people decreases the input.

Appoint a Facilitator for Each Group

This person monitors the rule-keeping and elicits response from the group to maintain and intensify the efforts. The facilitator may call on each participant to give an opinion or an idea, since full participation stimulates the group. From time to time it is well to change leadership to allow for a variety of styles and to provide experience in directing a session.

Take Short Recesses to Assure Maximal Productivity

This kind of thinking excites, but it also exhausts. It may even help to move the group to a new venue at the end of the generative process. In the new location the ban on criticism is eliminated and discriminating evaluation can take place. Selection of the best idea or a combination of good ideas must now be decided.

Evaluate the Ideas

Some concepts will be welcomed as is, but others can be improved. A few must be discarded. But in combination, many can be incorporated. Most importantly, all must be evaluated against the mission statement of your organization.

Always Commit to Implementation

Ask the question, What can we do to put these ideas to work? You may come up with a proposal, a model, a sketch, or a list of next steps and appoint a presentation team or a project coordinator. Disney World was seven years in the planning stages. Most of what became an international playground was accomplished by brainstorming.

Five Principles of Brainstorming

1. Stay focused on the topic.

2. Encourage wild ideas.

3. Defer Judgment.

4. Build on the ideas of others.

5. Allow one conversation at a time.

IDEO Company

Variations on Brainstorming

Mind-Storming

Individuals as well as groups may brainstorm. With a problem statement in front of you, push yourself to generate twenty solutions to the question at hand. Then try to implement at least one of them.

Paired Discussion

Use paired discussion when the energy level decreases in a group. Participation in twos or threes provides a mini-brainstorming experience, and the results may then be shared with the larger group. Sometimes this technique is effective for a multi-part plan in which persons of varying skills are participating.

Affinity Diagramming

Post-It notes (a trademark of 3M Company) supplies a means of writing ideas and sticking them on a flipchart for sorting. This means of thinking is a good anonymous way to get ideas that may be reluctantly given. For more group involvement, however, participants can repeat their ideas aloud as they hand them to the assistant for posting. Energy levels are apt to remain higher with ideas coming faster than the leader can write. Moreover, group members may take notes more easily.

Force Field Diagram

A more formal way to brainstorm is to create a diagram on a flipchart, with factors that motivate a particular change on the left side of the page, and those that hinder the change on the right. For the change to occur successfully, the driving motivational forces must be increased or decreased on either side.

After the introduction, the group suggests ways to enhance driving forces or to reduce restraints. Visual diagrams help people understand the relative weights of drivers and restrainers. This thinking of the problem in a different mode often yields new ideas.

Plussing

Plussing involves continually adding to a thing with a view to making it better and ultimately the best. This approach is recommended *after* brainstorming, as an accompaniment or follow-up. (For more on this subject see chapter 10.)

Lateral Thinking

Lateral thinking challenges people to think in new directions. The term was coined by Edward de Bono in his book of the same name.[2] Instead of thinking in a straight line, lateral thinkers "step to the side" and challenge themselves to think in a different way.

Ways Laypeople Can Assist a Pastor

The following ideas came from a brainstorming session in Columbus, Ohio, on March 5, 1991.

Praying for the pastor

Encouraging the pastor

Learning

Studying the Word

Leading an evangelistic Bible study

Supporting the pastor

Volunteering

Taking leadership

Sharing Christ with others

Being a disciple

Asking questions

Helping his family

Watching his children so he and his wife can get away

Giving the pastor money

Holding the pastor accountable for areas of his life

Changing places with the pastor for a day

Taking the pastor golfing

Reading for ideas to share with the pastor

Taking "busy work" off his hands when possible

Undertaking whatever he is burdened with

Giving constructive criticism and feedback

Asking the pastor what he is reading and learning

Being honest with the pastor

Intercepting calls and complaints

Providing a true friendship relationship

Listening to the pastor without offering comments

Try adding your own ideas!

Exercises

1. Would you like to try out the principles and practice of brainstorming? Here are some problem-statements you and your group can use for practice:
    - Improve our family Christmas celebration.
    - Develop a strategy to "spice up" our marriage.
    - Make our church user-friendly for the twenty-first century.
    - List ways to improve our church in the next one, five, and ten years.
    - Write a layperson's guide to making a pastor more efficient and effective.

2. Try this brainstorming exercise with a group of people—the larger, the better. Pass out one paper cup to every person in the room. Then give everyone two minutes to write down on a sheet of paper as many uses as they can think of for a paper cup. When time is up, ask for a show of hands to see how many uses people were able to list: Ten? Twenty? Twenty-five? Thirty? More?

    Next, divide the group into twos. Then give the groups two minutes to work together to come up with as many uses for a paper cup as they can (they are allowed to combine their previous lists). When time is up, ask for a show of hands to see how many uses the pairs were able to brainstorm together: Twenty? Thirty? Forty? More?

    Now appoint a recording secretary. Choosing one of the pairs at random, ask them to read aloud their entire list of ideas, while the secretary writes them down on a whiteboard or overhead transparency. When they are finished, ask another group to give you any additional ideas they have. Then ask the same of a third group, and so on until you have listed all the ideas from all the groups.

    When all the ideas of the entire group have been listed, ask if anyone has any more ideas as a result of hearing the ideas of the group.

    Finally, total up the number of ideas generated by your group. How does that total compare with the highest number of ideas generated by the pairs? How does it compare with the highest number generated by any single individual?

What does this exercise teach you about brainstorming?

Plussing

The commodity called creativity is much more universally distributed among the population than is usually supposed.

10

"If it ain't broke, don't fix it." Ever heard that? Don't believe it! Someone has overstated the case. If you buy into that principle, the United States would never have made it to the moon. Thomas Edison would never have invented the electric light bulb. Steve Jobs would never have developed the Macintosh computer. Why not? Because none of these were broken; they were nonexistent. Discovery and invention brought them into existence, because people challenged the status quo. The good can always be better, but the better must be superseded by the *best*.

How much in the evangelical church continues to exist because no one cares to find a better way? We are often confronted by a mania of mediocrity, rather than the challenge of change. The question is, Is that what we want? Every person called and used of God in every generation did not just keep on doing what he or she had always been doing. They altered their thinking and action, and the results were radical.

So it is in every generation. Jesus Christ Himself serves as the most dramatic example of a radical breakthrough. He came to "fulfill the Law" (Matt. 5:17). God's divine plussing did away with animal sacrifices when Christ died as the perfect satisfaction for sin. He rewrote the terms of personal righteousness. He demanded that we think differently about His kingdom.

As Christians our destiny is to be "like Christ." Our lives, therefore, must reflect an aura of positive newness if we are to be authentic Christians. Think of the incredible advances in the Industrial Revolution, and since then in the technology of our Information Age. Our challenge is to be like Christ in an unstable culture extremely at odds with His teachings.

The Origin and Definition of Plussing

Disneyland and Disney World would never have been completed at a world-class level if it were not for this technique. While Walt Disney did not invent it, he made it a viable instrument for quality work. Today it is used in a variety of settings.

> **"In 1995, companies filed for trademark protection on more than 175,000 product names—double the number ten years ago."**
>
> —Fast Company

Plussing involves continually adding to a thing with a view to making it better and ultimately the best. It demands a "holy dissatisfaction." That was essentially Paul's mentality in Philippians 3:12–13. He said, in effect, "I haven't arrived. I'm not perfect. I'm pressing on." When did he say that? Almost at the end of his life—the time when most people are sliding for home, reaching for the bench, talking about retirement. But not Paul. Certainly after his arduous ministry (2 Cor. 11:23–28), he was entitled to rest on his laurels and enjoy some well-earned down-time. Instead, he burned with a passion to reach a goal, "to win the prize for which God has called me heavenward in Christ Jesus" (Phil. 3:14).

The Creative Thinking System

Walt Disney used what he called the Creative Thinking System. Here are the four components:

The Creative Thinking System

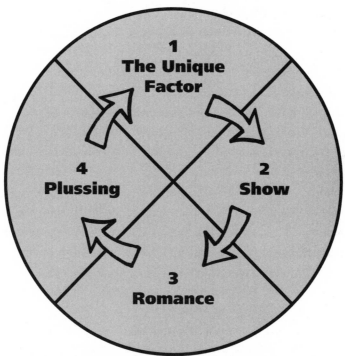

1. *The unique factor.* The major objective in the creative thinking system is the development and discovery of the "unique factor." It's important not to copy what other people do but through creative thought to develop a unique approach. Great success stories result from the discovery of a singular factor.
2. *The show factor.* Do what you do so well that people will want to show others how well you do it. This objective is accomplished by devotion to excellence and refusing to sanction incompetence.
3. *The romance factor.* Romance the idea or concept and raise it to a new standard. Add that special touch to it! Walt Disney romanced the amusement park and created a new thing—the theme park.
4. *The plussing factor.* Never let something alone. Keep fooling around with it, improving it, and making it better. You know you have a unique factor when someone steals it. So keep the unique factor unique by constantly plussing it.

The Uses of Plussing

Plussing can be useful in many areas. In the communication area continue to improve your teaching and preaching, both in content and form. Effective communicators never stop developing their skills.

Attempt to equip new church members to function more effectively in their involvement in your local church. After each class, secure feedback from the participants to determine how you can "plus" the experience.

Each year many churches promote a variety of events—Bible conferences, a missionary week, family retreats, and the like. The key to excellence in each event is to evaluate during and after each one to determine what's missing, what can be done better, what can be added, and what needs to be omitted.

Learn to celebrate anniversaries, graduations, baptisms, outstanding accomplishments, and other rites of passage. Nearly every aspect of Christian mission has something that can be emphasized and/or enlarged in a creative way to make the message of Christ more effective.

Ideathematic

If I give you a dollar bill
And you give one to me
We each will have a dollar still
That's not much gain, you see . . .

If I give you a new idea
And I get one of yours
Now each of us has two because
Ideas are double doers.

—*Jack Moss, Moss Key-Rec Systems, Dayton, Ohio*

Exercises

1. Here are some ideas you can use to practice plussing:
   - How can a layperson help a pastor be more effective?
   - What can we change to make our ministry more attractive to the unreached?
   - Evaluate each age level from the nursery to the seniors in your church's ministry with a view to plussing.
   - What bridges with your community can be widened or strengthened?
2. First individually, and then with a group, come up with five ideas for innovations that would improve the quality, efficiency, or effectiveness of some of the following products, services, or processes: the toothbrush, the TV remote control, placing an order over the phone, delivery of your daily newspaper, boarding or deboarding a commercial jetliner, seminary education.

Five-Sensing

A cookie store is a bad idea. Besides, the market research reports say America likes crispy cookies, not soft and chewy cookies like you make.

—Rejection Letter To Debbi Fields, Founder of Mrs. Fields Cookies

11

Five-sensing is the language of our esthetic nature. Most formal education leans strongly toward the visual and auditory means of communicating information. Our eyes and ears do most of the work. But there are three other senses—smell, taste, and touch. If we ignore them, we starve them.

People are able to relate what they already know and what they observe through their senses to find relevancy where they did not see it before. When Jesus taught, He used each of the five senses, and everything around Him, as learning channels. The world was His classroom. He took advantage of every situation and all of people's faculties.

I find it curious that Jesus was the ultimate Teacher, yet He had none of the modern technology and teaching tools available to us. He was continuously creative in His instruction, applying truth to the real world of His day. So it's fair to ask, If our Lord did what He did with what He had, what should we be able to do with the methods, tools, and knowledge available to us today?

Studies show that people tend to remember only about 10 percent of what they hear, 50 percent of what they hear and see, but 90 percent of what they hear, see, and do. The senses bring raw materials to the mind, but the way the mind processes observations is influenced by one's past experiences, purpose, and attitudes. In other words, the eyes see, but the mind organizes. Therefore the more we use all five senses, the greater the learning and the more permanent the retention.

Five-sensing and plussing are both spinoffs of brainstorming. As education increases, imagination often decreases. Five-sensing is a conscious effort to think with all the senses about how a given event or presentation can communicate sensually with the ones receiving the message.

The power of this technique was shown dramatically in the life of Helen Keller, a blind, deaf-mute girl born in Alabama in 1880. When her parents appealed to Alexander Graham Bell for counsel, he found Anne Sullivan, an extraordinary twenty-year-old teacher. She herself had formerly been blind, but was partially cured, and was a graduate of the Perkins School for the Blind in Boston.

Within a month of working with Helen, Anne Sullivan had imparted the gift of language to her seven-year-old pupil. Under her constant instruction, Helen Keller not only learned to speak, read, and write but became exceptionally proficient in standard studies. She entered Radcliffe University in 1900, graduated four years later magna cum laude, and, using her creative abilities, left a legacy of ten major books.

How could this seeming miracle possibly have come about? Under the hard bony structure of the skull lies a section of the brain scientists call the parietal lobe. This "feeling" part of the brain contains the sensory cortex, which receives impulses from all the sensory receptors. Specific touch is centered here. This is not to say that we do not feel pain or pressure lower in the body, but it cannot be localized unless this section of the brain is functioning.

Next, in a downward direction of the brain lies the temporal lobe, the area involving hearing and memory. And somewhat behind that is the visual center. Now think downward to the brain stem, that extension of the spinal cord which receives information from the various parts of the body. Here is the center for all the senses except smell and vision. These two exceptions connect directly with the limbic system and the cerebral cortex, which controls our highest conceptual and motor functions. Perhaps this accounts for why they have such a powerful effect on us.[1]

The Five Senses

Sight

This involves any form of visualization. The Bible includes many examples of God's use of the visual to teach important truths: the rainbow for Noah, the burning bush for Moses, lightning for the psalmist, the rent veil of the temple for the Jews of Jesus' day. Today, the multimedia revolution has introduced a variety of new ways to see: whiteboards, posters, overhead projectors, photographs, slides, films, 3-D models, videos, and so on. In all these technologies, a principle remains: Sight is a faculty; seeing is an art.

Hearing

This involves any acoustical expression. Music, radio broadcasts, audio-cassette tapes, CDs, television, movies, and dramatic presentations all use sound for effective impact. One has only to visit the Walt Disney studios to learn of enormous developments in this area of communication. Thunder, the song of a bird, the wind in a canyon, and the countless other noises of nature all illustrate the importance God places on sound.

Taste

Taste is an overlooked resource for effective communication in most churches today. But it was not always so for God's people. Consider events like the manna in the wilderness, or the Passover meal, which used bitter herbs to remind the Israelites of the bitterness of Egypt. The New Testament counterpart which we call the Lord's Supper also exemplifies God's use of taste in teaching spiritual truth. (In light of this, it's legitimate to ask why the communion elements of many churches often taste so bland. Is that the sense we want to connect with the meaning of the Lord's Supper?)

Touch

A simple handshake, an embrace, or even a light pat on the shoulder conveys a feeling unlike any other. Kids with hands-on experiences do not have to be told, "Don't touch that!" In nature the elements of cool water, warm sunshine, and bitter wind, among many others, remind us of the importance of this sense. Notice how frequently Jesus touched people when He healed them.

Smell

In biblical settings this sense was almost always combined with others—for example, with touch in baptism, with taste in the Passover and Lord's Supper, and with spices in ancient Christian burials. Aged and blind Isaac identified his sons by their smell, and the woman who bathed Jesus' feet with perfume utilized the beauty of smell.

A Christian Tradition of Five-Sensing

From its earliest days the Christian church has employed a combination of sensory devices for worship and instruction. The very architecture of a church building often defines visually much of its belief system. Obviously Christians can worship God anywhere—inside or out-of-doors, in homes or in catacombs, on the street or on an airplane. But beautiful and symbolic churches provide esthetic assistance.

Early on, believers worshiped in nontraditional places. But when Emperor Constantine made Christianity the official religion of the Roman Empire, the need for secrecy was gone, and Christianity began to employ the rectangular hall of the Roman basilica as a meeting place. Divided into three sections by two rows of columns parallel with the longer sides, this form of building had a semicircular "apse" that opened from one of the shorter sides. The roof provided windows through which light could enter.

From this original pattern, two other types developed. In the East, Byzantine churches included martyrions (where relics of martyrs were buried) and domed roofs. In the West, Gothic arches and a ground plan in the form of a cross were built to express visually important concepts for worshipers. Impressive church buildings reflected the prestige of Christianity in the nineteenth century. Our contemporary styles now show a concern to make buildings functional to meet the needs of the modern world.

Christianity is rooted in the present and in reality, as opposed to remote or fanciful history. It is not a retreat from the real, historical, human experience, but rather the redemption and glorification of that existence. The doctrines of Creation and Incarnation quite naturally celebrate human flesh, created in the image of God, made for the habitation of the incarnate Word, and redeemed for eternal life.

We must remember that before Gutenberg's invention of the printing press and the subsequent production of books, most people were relatively unschooled. They had little access to written materials. Therefore apart from the preaching and teaching of learned scholars, art stood as the chief method for teaching the facts and implications of Christian truth.

Under these circumstances the human imagination was roused to reflect on the intangible concepts of the gospel and render them in more tangible expressions, using shape, color, perspective, and a myriad of other visual means, along with musical, narrative, and dramatic forms. No single thread binds Christian art forms over sixteen hundred years. Sir Christopher Wren's Westminster Abbey in London is quite different from Chartres Cathedral. The icon of the Virgin of Vladimir in Russia differs greatly from Rembrandt's painting of the Holy Family.

Christians have always differed on the question of what sort of imagery is appropriate. One has only to look at the disparity in Christmas cards to understand the many ways artists look at our faith. Over the centuries, believers have learned through travel, art, craft, games, drama, sculpture, poetry, various rites, and an endless array of music and narrative literature.

Consider, for example, two often-used means in our own Christian community: excursions to the Holy Land and short-term visits to overseas mission fields. These well illustrate the combination of alerting all the senses to the realism of our message and our Lord's mandate to take the gospel to the entire world.

Yet there remains a critical need for creative expression in our current technological society. While we may think of the medieval world as mystical, our own climate needs truth presented creatively more than ever. Professor H. R. Rookmaker contends, "There is no age as mystical as ours. Yet it is a mysticism with a difference: It is a nihilistic mysticism, for God is dead. Very old ideas are being revived; gnosticism, neo-platonic ideas of reality emanating from and returning to God, and eastern religion, a religion with a god that is not a god but impersonal and universalistic, a god which (not who!) is everything and therefore nothing, with a salvation that is in the end self-annihilation."[2]

Christians have always used imagination, as did our Lord, in teaching. We are reminded by Julian of Norwich that "The one thing that matters is that we always say 'yes' to God whenever we experience Him."

Exercises

1. Try highlighting every use of the senses in your personal Bible study.
2. Plan a celebration using a combination of all five sensual triggers.
3. Use the technique of brainstorming to devise creative ways to develop each of your own senses that you underuse, particularly smell, taste, and touch.
4. Answer this question: How could we improve our celebration of Christmas using five-sensing?
5. Use the techniques of brainstorming and plussing to devise more effective ways, using five-sensing, to teach the basics of Christianity to newcomers in a New Members or Discovery class, or a Bible study or discipleship group.
6. How could a senior citizens' group use five-sensing to enhance their fellowship?

Objection-Countering

640K ought to be enough for anybody.

—BILL GATES, 1981

12

I remember hearing my grandmother in family conversations where I, as a young boy, was the subject of discussion. Because she had the sensitivity to think like a little child, she would staunchly defend my rights and propose alternative ways to relieve a given tension. Her methods come to mind in considering the matter of creative objection-countering.

A process of vicarious thinking, this technique fosters the ability to climb into the skin of another, so to speak, to read the brain of the person you are trying to reach—the customer, the Sunday-school student, the non-Christian. It is an especially useful skill in communicating with unchurched individuals and with groups or populations typically uninterested in church, such as members of Generation X.

Objection-countering also facilitates the evaluation process in weeding out or plussing ideas. It aids in resolving the quandaries of how to take an idea that is weak or of questionable value and transform it into a superior strategy for implementation.

> **"This 'telephone' has too many shortcomings to be seriously considered as a means of communication. The device is inherently of no value to us."**
>
> —*Western Union Internal Memo, 1876*

Using Objection-Countering in the Church

Each year every program in our churches and ministries should have to stand trial for its life on the basis of biblical objectives, relevance to our mission, and practical effectiveness. We need to ask, Is this still our commitment? Is it still working well?

Consider these illustrations from five common areas of ministry.

Evangelism

Search Ministries took on the assignment of reaching the unreached for Christ primarily by utilizing the technique of objection-countering. In their research they discovered that modern-day resistance to the gospel generally boils down to twelve basic questions, in some variation or combination. They recognized their challenge, then, as the need to respond intelligently to these questions from a biblical perspective. (The answers they came up with are summarized in a fine book, *I'm Glad You Asked*, by Ken Boa and Larry Moody [Colorado Springs: ChariotVictor, 1994].)

Search's set of questions is arranged from the general to the specific. The first three are objections to religion itself, the next five are objections to Christianity in particular, and the final four are problems specifically related to salvation by faith in Christ. This excellent aid to ministry is designed to equip Christians to implement the principle of 1 Peter 3:15, of being ready to give answers for the hope within us. This mental preparation engenders confidence and helps one become an able defender and promoter of the faith.

Education

One of the major challenges of working with Christian high-school students is to prepare them for the humanistic secularism of higher education.

Probe Ministries has addressed this harsh reality by going into the university setting with a view toward objection-countering. Probe researched the seminal issues that confront the Christian student, then came up with a set of precollege workshops to prepare students for the learning experience to come.

Studies have revealed that exposing a person to a hostile philosophy in a friendly, favorable setting, prior to the reality, takes the sting out of later real-life confrontation. When people meet opposition unprepared, they tend to be shocked by the experience and feel inadequate to cope. But by role-playing ahead of time, they come to the moment with greater confidence, since they know what to expect.

Reaching the Unchurched

How do we reach the average person in our postmodern society who seems to care nothing about spiritual issues? For example, A factory worker addicted to carnal appetites? A "couch potato" hooked on vacuous television? A businessman consumed with his golf game? A success-driven professional? A frustrated and exhausted single mother? A gang-savvy teenager?

These are the kinds of people who populate your community (and mine). What are we doing to reach them? What creativity are we putting into answering that question?

Objection-countering is a way to plug into the thinking of such individuals and to ask, from their perspective, How can we invade their territory? What magnet will draw them away from their addictions, agendas, and allegiances, at least long enough to consider seriously what Jesus Christ has to offer them?

Christian Business and Professional People

In a survey conducted in the Dallas/Fort Worth area, more than twenty-five hundred Christian business and professional people were asked, "What connection do you see between what happens in your church on Sunday morning and what transpires in your office on Monday morning?" The overwhelming response was, "Little or none."

This led to the use of the objection-countering technique, using another survey. The same people were asked to list real-world issues for which they felt their church was not preparing them. Here's a list of the "critical issues" they identified. It could well serve as an agenda for the teaching and training programs of your congregation or organization.

109 Critical Issues

1. Adversity, coping
2. Alcoholism/drug abuse
3. Ambition
4. Anger
5. Anxiety/job security
6. Balancing competing issue demands
7. Bankruptcy
8. Bitterness
9. Boredom
10. Bribes and kickbacks
11. Business with Christians
12. Career planning
13. Career selection
14. Communication/speech
15. Communication/salary
16. Competition
17. Complaining
18. Compromise, dynamics of
19. Conflict resolution
20. Confrontation of Christians
21. Conscience/how to follow
22. Criticism, taking it/ giving it
23. Deception
24. Decision-making and problem-solving skills
25. Disillusionment
26. Domination and control
27. Ego/pride/security
28. Entertaining and social involvements with clients/coworkers
29. Entrapment/frustration
30. Ethics in business
31. Excellence
32. Failure
33. Fairness
34. Faithfulness, contracts, and promises
35. Fatigue/loss of energy
36. Femininity and business values
37. Finances (business)
38. Finances (personal)
39. Firing
40. Flexibility
41. Fulfillment in work
42. Greed
43. Guilt for not going into the ministry
44. Honesty
45. Idolatry
46. Image
47. Income/lifestyle
48. Incorporating
49. Inspiring moral excellence in others
50. Integrity
51. Jealousy, envy
52. Joy/happiness
53. Lack of meaning at work
54. Lawsuits and retaliation
55. Leadership
56. Leisure and rest
57. Loneliness
58. Materialism
59. Midlife crisis
60. Mistakes, what they teach you
61. Motherhood and your career
62. Motivation
63. Motives for work
64. Narcissism
65. Negotiating
66. Overwork/workaholism
67. Partiality
68. Participation in evil
69. Partnerships
70. Peer pressure
71. Perfectionism
72. Perseverance
73. Philosophy of business, biblical
74. Philosophy of management
75. Planning
76. Politicking
77. Priorities
78. Profit motive
79. Relating to non-Christians at work
80. Relationships with competitors
81. Relationships with customers
82. Relationships with enemies
83. Relationships with government
84. Relationships with peers
85. Relationships with subordinates
86. Relationships with superiors
87. Relationships, healthy male/female at work
88. Reputation
89. Retirement

109 Critical Issues (Cont'd)

90. Risk-taking	97. Stress from pleasing people	105. Whistle-blowing
91. Self-betrayal	98. Success	106. Working women, career goals
92. Service/servant attitude toward customers/clients	99. Talent, using it for the cause of Christ	107. Working women, dealing with male attitudes
93. Sexual immorality in the workplace	100. Time management	108. Working women, tension between work and family
94. Significance/self-esteem	101. Travel, problems of	109. Working women, tradeoffs
95. Stress from busyness	102. Unemployment	
96. Stress from finances	103. Union involvement	
	104. Upward mobility	

Exit Interviews

By some accounts the evangelical church is booming with growth. Baby boomers who left church in the sixties and seventies appear to be returning, bringing their children (and their money) with them. As a result, megachurches—congregations of a thousand or more people—seem to spring up overnight in areas where few churches even existed before.

Yet while countless people may be flocking in the front door of churches today, a steady stream of disillusioned Christians is quietly flowing out the back. Observing this overlooked trend, my son Bill thought to ask the critical question, Why? To find out, he used a form of objection-countering known as the exit interview. He found several dozen "back-door believers," folks who had walked away from church. He invited them to tell their story, guaranteeing anonymity.

The result was the book *Exit Interviews: Revealing Stories of Why People Are Leaving the Church* (Chicago: Moody, 1993). The interviews make for fascinating reading. They also enabled Bill to make a number of interesting observations that ought to stick like knives in the brain of every church leader.

- It is not newcomers who are leaving the churches but the old-timers, people who have been in the faith and in the church—some even in the ministry—for ten, twenty, or even thirty or more years.
- Most of those interviewed had not left the faith; they had left the community of faith. In other words, they were not giving up on the Lord, but they had given up on churches that, in their perception, had failed them.

- Most viewed their departure as temporary. They could foresee a time when they would probably reengage with a congregation, so long as it was the "right" congregation.
- When people decide to leave, they don't immediately go elsewhere. They go into a "holding pattern," waiting for about six to eight weeks for someone from their former church to contact them. If no one does, they then start looking around for other options. Bill found that 100 percent of the people he interviewed had never received a call from their church. Most of them told Bill that he was the first person who had *ever* asked them why they had left the church.
- The reasons people left were not particularly mysterious. Among the explanations: lack of a relevant message, lack of or failure of community life, trouble connecting with God through what the church had to offer, failure to identify the person's giftedness or utilize it in a meaningful way. Very basic stuff.

What could you learn by strategically applying the exit-interview technique (or its relative, the focus group)? You have to be willing to listen, to hear people tell it like it is, warts and all. But imagine what you could gain by using exit interviews to:

- Identify opportunities (which, by the way, tend to be disguised as problems) in your worship services.
- Gain feedback on a particular sermon or a series of messages.
- Evaluate the effectiveness of your adult Sunday-school program.
- Troubleshoot a longstanding program that seems to be slipping in popularity.
- Learn how your church is perceived by the surrounding community.

"Television won't be able to hold onto any market it captures after the first six months. People will soon get tired of staring at a plywood box every night."

—*Daryl F. Zanuck, head of 20th Century Fox, 1946*

Objection-countering has infinite applications. It can be something as simple as asking people to write anonymously on a 3" x 5" card, three things that are kicking the slats out of their lives. This could provide more insight for a pastor or teacher of a Bible class than any other technique—and it's very nonthreatening.

I have conducted such a card survey with several groups of seminary students over a period of time. My question: "If you could ask only one question before being graduated from seminary, what would it be?" Again, this was done without identification. The results were staggering—and informative!

It may be that we continue to answer questions no one is asking, but the things that devastate lives we never get around to discussing.

Exercises

1. Use the principles of objection-countering to create responses to the following statements that are often heard when new ideas are suggested:
    *   "We've always done it this way."
    *   "That will take too much time/energy/money/etc."
    *   "That's not really your responsibility."
    *   "We've tried that before and it didn't work."
    *   "Why try something new if what we've got is working okay?"
    *   "Let's not rock the boat."
2. Review the list of 109 critical issues in this chapter. Select one or a handful of items from the list and ask, How could our church devise ways to help our people deal with these issues?
3. Survey a dozen people in your neighborhood or workplace. Ask them if they go to church. If they do, ask them to name the best thing about their church, and then ask them to name the one thing they would do to make their church better. If they don't go to church, ask them to name the one thing they'd most want in a church if they did go to church.

Helpful Resources

- Boa, Ken, and Larry Moody. *I'm Glad You Asked.* Colorado Springs: ChariotVictor, 1994.
- Hendricks, William. *Exit Interviews: Revealing Stories of Why People Are Leaving the Church.* Chicago: Moody Press, 1993.

Probe Ministries, 1900 Firman Drive, Suite 100, Richardson, TX 75081
Tel: 972-480-0240
Fax: 972-644-9664

Search Ministries, 5038 Dorsey Hall Drive, Ellicott City, MD 21042
Tel: 410-740-5300
Fax: 410-740-5305

Walk Thru the Bible Ministries, 4201 N. Peachtree Road, Atlanta, GA 30341-1362
Tel: 770-458-9300
Fax: 770-454-9313

Gaming

Babe Ruth struck out nearly twice as often as he hit home runs.

—A BASEBALL FACT

13

The American mind-set tends to relegate games to the relaxed, recreational side of life. Most of us have played games all our lives, but in the process an educational fallout has occurred. For it turns out that far more than fun is happening when we play games; our thinking processes are actually undergoing fundamental development. For example, decision-making and problem-solving skills may be required by our play. Strategy is invariably demanded. Inventiveness may also be involved. This makes the use of games a valuable creative tool in our task of proclaiming the gospel to the world.

Kinds of Gaming

There are two broad categories of gaming—competition and simulation. Competition is a common type of game that follows a well-defined set of rules to win over opposition. A wide variety of competitive games, puzzles, and toys exist that can develop mental flexibility—a crucial element in the growth of one's creativity. Competitive skill can be used individually (as in crossword puzzles or a Rubik's cube) or with others (as in checkers, chess, and Monopoly).

Children who are reared on competitive contests like these tend to score higher on problem-solving tests. Habit patterns formed early in life can be gradually developed with games of greater sophistication.

Games of simulation try to reproduce some form of reality in order to seek a solution to a given problem. Major law schools employ this form of gaming by their use of case studies. One oft-cited instance at Harvard Law School placed students in the position of CEO of a multinational corporation. For weeks, theoretical solutions were posed for real problems. At the conclusion of the study, the professor opened the door to introduce the real-life CEO, who proceeded to inform the class of how inaccurately they had assessed and resolved dilemmas he was actually facing.

With simulation, judgmental errors are not fatal. The game becomes a practice run for later, real-life experience.

> **"Videogames are perfect training for life in America, where daily existence demands the ability to parse sixteen kinds of information being fired at you simultancously from telephones, televisions, fax machines, pagers, personal digital assistants, voice messaging systems, postal delivery, office e-mail, and the Internet."**
>
> —*J. C. Hertz*, Joystick Nation

Numerous references in the Scriptures alert us to the historical practice of playing games. When Jonah fled from the Lord, the terrified sailors on his Tarshish-bound ship cast lots to learn their fate (Jonah 1:7). Similarly the soldiers at the foot of the cross where Jesus died cast lots for His clothing (Matt. 27:35). These were both games of chance. Jesus referred to children's games as He contrasted two groups of those who criticized Him (11:16–17). Games, common to all people, provide an idea flint on which to strike creative sparks. The creation of play makes learning exciting.

A Definition of Gaming

Gaming is a branch of mathematics that aims to analyze various problems of conflict by abstracting "models," or games. By stressing strategic aspects, controlled by the participants, gaming goes beyond the classical theory of probability. It is a kind of language for describing competitive strategies the players, under prescribed rules, can use to form coalitions that thwart the activities of others.

In the creative process gaming achieves educational and spiritual objectives. Used extensively in the military, leadership development seminars, and rehabilitation centers, the process organizes thinking by setting free common inhibitions. Games minimize risk by reducing reality to a manageable object or role play. In a Christian framework we need to be wary of seeing others as competitors. Our primary competition is with ourselves to become all that God created us to be.

Exercises

Here are some games to provide practice in creativity development.

The Communication Game

Divide a group into teams of five members each. Any extra members of the group are asked to "float" quietly, observing and eventually reporting back their observations to the whole group at the end of the exercise.

The key objectives of the game are cooperation and competition in fitting together pieces of puzzles. Each group of five must cooperate *nonverbally* in order to compete against other groups of five. Each person receives an envelope containing some pieces of cardboard of various shapes. These shapes are to be shared among each group of five so that, at the completion of the exercise, each member of the group has a completed square in front of him or her. The pieces will fit together in many ways, but there is only one arrangement possible for all five group members to have uniform squares completed. The rules are as follows:

1. The task of each person in the group is to form a square. All five squares in the group must be the same size.
2. Each person is to work directly on his own square only, not on those of the other teammates.

3.   A person may give pieces to another person but may not take or motion for pieces from anyone else unless they are offered.

4.   No talking or gesturing is allowed, and each person must keep his pieces directly in front of him or her.

5.   The first group with all five squares completed is the winner and may watch the other groups (but not talk).

6.   The factors that helped or hindered in completing the squares are to be kept in mind for discussion following the exercise.

Preparation: The large squares should be cut as shown below. Then distribute them randomly into five envelopes, with no complete square being contained in any one envelope. Prepare a set of five envelopes for each group.

A Biblical Brain Teaser

Can you find sixteen books of the Bible hidden in the following paragraph?

I once made a remark about the hidden books of the Bible. It was a lulu. Kept people looking so hard for facts and for others it was a revelation. Some were in a jam, especially since the names of the books were not capitalized: But the truth finally struck home to numbers of readers. To others it was a real job. We want it to be a most fascinating few moments for you. YES, THERE WILL BE SOME REALLY EASY ONES TO SPOT. Others may require judges to help them. I will quickly admit it usually takes a minister to find one of them, and there will be loud lamentations when it is found. A little lady says she brews a cup of tea so she can concentrate better. See how well you can compete. Relax now, for there are really sixteen names of the books of the Bible in this story.

(One person found fifteen books in twenty minutes. But it took him *three weeks* to find the sixteenth!)

How Many Squares?

How many squares are in the diagram below?

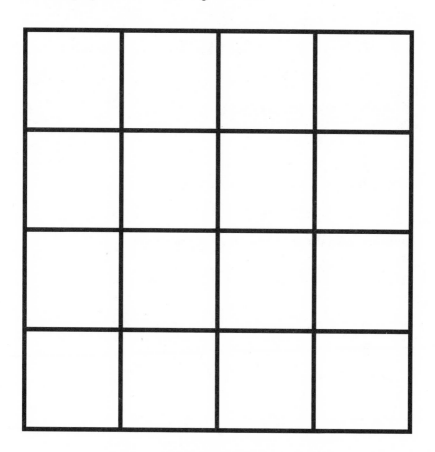

Helpful Resources

- Fluegelman, Andrew, ed. *The New Games Book.* Berkeley, CA: Headlands Press, n.d.
- Michalko, Michael. *Tinkertoys.* Berkeley, CA: Ten Speed Press, 1991.
- Rohnke, Karl. *Cowstails and Cobras.* Project Adventure, P.O. Box 157, Hamilton, MA 01936. Tel: 617-468-1766.

- Wujec, Tom. *Five Star Mind: Games and Puzzles to Stimulate Your Creativity and Imagination.* New York: Doubleday & Co., 1995.

New Games Foundation, P.O. Box 7901, San Francisco, CA 94120
Tel: 415-824-6900

Simile II, Box 910, Del Mar, CA 92014
Tel: 619-755-0272
This company produces a fine catalog of simulation games.

Benjy Simpson, *Initiative Games,* Colorado Outward Bound Schools, Publications Secretary, 945 Pennsylvania Street, Denver, CO 80203-3198.
Tel: 303-837-0880
This book is highly recommended. Also ask for the *Colorado Outward Bound Instructor's Manual,* an excellent source for games and rope courses.

University Associates, 8517 Production Avenue, San Diego, CA 92121
Tel: 619-578-5900
Ask for their *HRD Resource Guide.* It's the best!

Mind-Mapping

The learning challenge faced by all of us [is] to continually expand our awareness and understanding, to see more of the interdependencies between actions and reality, to see more and more of our connectedness to the world around us.

—PETER SENGE

14

Mind-mapping is a creative way to take notes, generate ideas, or organize information. Quick and visual, mind-maps help participants conceptualize. Their purpose is to outline the elements of a large problem, concept, or topic in a free-form manner, based on the way neural networks are designed. Some successful uses include developing business plans and designing training sessions.

Mind-mapping works particularly well with people brought together from different backgrounds, or who do not know each other. For individuals, it serves as a personal tool when one is thinking through a question or planning a strategy.

Mind-mapping begins with a blank sheet of paper—preferably large, since physical boundaries tend to hinder the process. For groups, several pieces of flipchart paper together can make a wall-sized sheet. In the middle of the paper, draw a circle and write the problem statement or topic inside it. Using lines radiating from the circle, connect other circles containing the main concepts or ideas related to the core issue. Use capital letters and distinctive colors for the important concepts.

Keep generating additional ideas and thoughts, linking subordinate items to the greater ones. As the mind-map evolves, there will be a vast network of interconnected circles, all of which relate directly or indirectly to the core circle. By the way, it helps to draw pictures or symbols to illustrate key ideas.

Pierce J. Howard describes the mind-mapping process this way: (1) Circle the central topic in the center of the page. (2) Put associated topics in bubbles with connecting lines. (3) To each subtopic connect additional related elements. (4) Use bolder lines, squiggly lines, shading colors, and so forth to identify levels of topics.[1]

1. Circle the central topic in the center of the page.

2. Put associated topics in bubbles with connecting lines.

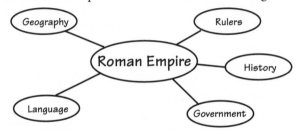

3. To each subtopic, connect additional related elements.

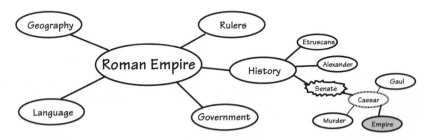

4. Use bolder lines, squiggly lines, shading, colors, and so on to identify levels of topics.

Here's an example of how mind-mapping works. Say you are planning a missions conference and want to organize everything you will need. In the middle of a sheet of paper, you would write "missions conference" and draw a circle around it. Then you might draw several lines out from that circle and connect them to other circles in which you might write in capital letters and different colors words like "location," "AV equipment," "guest speakers," "promotion," "housing," and so forth.

From the AV equipment circle, you might draw some new lines and add items such as "overhead projector," "cassette recorder," "TV/VCR," and "tape player." From there, another branch might grow to include "screen," "extra bulbs," "extension cords," "pertinent tapes," and so on.

After completing a mind-map, hang it in a central location in order for participants to review it regularly and refresh their memories—and also to add things they overlooked. And when the map has outlived its immediate usefulness, don't just throw it away; file it so that the next planning committee can profit from your process and not have to start from scratch.

Exercises

1. Use mind-mapping to think through one of the following:
   - Your high schooler is preparing for college education. What does he or she need to consider?
   - The people in your office need better communication. What's the system for communicating now? Who communicates with whom? How? What would you *like* the communication system to look like?
   - Your elderly parent needs elder-care. What are all the factors that need to be considered?
   - You have a year's worth of Bible teaching to plan. Some of it you will give in sermons, some of it in adult Sunday-school classes, and some of it in Bible studies and other small-group forums. What passages, issues, and topics would you like to cover, and what are the relationships between the various teaching venues?
2. Have you ever put off thinking about a problem or issue because you have the attitude, "I'm not in the mood yet"? Mind-mapping is one way to get your brain (and your motivation) jump-started. For one thing, mind-mapping can shorten the amount of time

required for thinking. It also helps you overcome stress. So try mind-mapping the next time you feel "stuck" over one of the following:

- scheduling
- introducing change into your organization
- coming up with a name for a program or title for a publication
- generating new ideas for sermons or Bible lessons
- defining goals
- making a decision
- figuring out what you want in life

Helpful Resources

- Buzan, Tony, and Barry Buzan. *The Mind Map Book.* New York: E. P. Dutton, 1994.
- Wycoff, Joy. *Mindmapping: Your Personal Guide to Exploring Creativity and Problem-Solving.* New York: Berkley Publishing Group, 1991.

Roles

The real world of work consists mostly of horizontal relationships. Most of the people you see from day to day don't work for you, and you don't work for them. You work together, even if that isn't the way it looks on the chart.

—HARLAN CLEVELAND

15

Roger von Oech, in his refreshingly provocative book *A Kick in the Seat of the Pants*, suggests four roles for a creator.[1] Not four different kinds of people, but four different roles that *every* person needs to learn to exercise his or her creative activity. Everyone has natural strengths and weaknesses. The strengths need to be exploited, and the weaknesses enriched. Here are the four roles.

The Explorer

This person is often a collector of stuff. He goes to places he has never been before, eats foods new to him, meets people he has never met before, reads new books. He probes into fields of interest and activity never before experienced, keying in on the diversity of people, places, and things.

The value of this exploratory activity is that it exposes a person to the new, the different, and the unexpected. It keeps his mind from getting into the ruts of well-worn paths. It also helps him avoid the "been there, done that" attitude that is like acid to creative possibilities.

The Artist

This role always has the person asking, "What can I make with this?" The artist often uses original materials and/or design to craft a model, paint a picture, write a song, compose a poem, or decorate a room. He is constantly seeking to engender and embellish some new and different object or combination with his own touch of creativity.

The value of this role is its expressiveness. Too many good ideas stay locked up in the brain as abstractions. The artist brings vision to life. And his vision helps rearrange the world into more interesting, beautiful, and effective combinations.

The Judge

Here is the critical thinking role. The judge is a person with a question mark for a brain. "What good is this?" "How much will it cost?" "How long will it take?" "Will it last?"

For some reason, our Western world has produced more judges than artists or explorers. This may be the result of our educational system, which was set up to prepare people for work in factories and large organizations. There are signs that things are now changing to fit the times. However, as they do, we must never lose sight of the crucial need for critical thinking.

Critical thinking is anathema at the front end of the creative process. Newborn ideas, like infants, are essentially powerless. They need protection in their infancy, as they struggle to grow into viability. Harsh criticism too early can quickly kill a promising concept.

Later on, however, judgment is indispensable, because not all ideas are good ideas. Indeed, out of a hundred ideas, maybe five are pretty good, and only one or two are really exceptional. Before we move *any* idea into the implementation stage, we need critical thinkers to ask it (and its implementers) some tough questions. Otherwise we can end up with a fiasco, with people asking, "Whose crazy idea was this, anyway?!" The problem, of course, is not with the origin of the idea but with its lack of review.

The Warrior

This is the role for action. "It's where the rubber meets the road," as they say. People acting in this role include salesmen, classroom teachers, athletes, emergency medical technicians, and certain entrepreneurs. These are folks on the delivery end of creativity. "That idea sounds pretty good," they are liable to say, "but let's not talk about, let's *do* it!"

One persistent question nags the warrior: "Is this idea doable . . . worthwhile . . . cost-productive . . . saleable? Will it work?" These are folks with a graduate degree from the school of hard knocks. They are indispensable to the creative process because sooner or later, ideas have to connect with real life. Warriors help make that connection.

Which Role Are You?

Ideally, all of us need to take on all four of these roles somewhere along the way. However, by virtue of our natural bent, we tend to favor one role more than the others. Discovering that role will help us know where our best contribution can be made to the creative process.

Our self-evaluation needs to include an objective answer to the questions, "What are my strengths," and "What are my weaknesses?" Von Oech suggests that these ideas will grow on each of us like an old friend, and as we ponder them, our creativity will grow.

Exercises

1. If you are on a board, committee, or team, think about the individuals in your group. Which roles does each person tend to play? Ask each of them which roles *they* feel they play, and which one(s) they would *like* to play? Based on their responses, how could you organize and align your group for the greatest effectiveness?
2. Next time your group is trying to solve a problem, brainstorm an idea, or create a new set of goals or direction, use the role-playing strategy described above to channel everyone's creativity. Spend twenty minutes looking at the situation from the standpoint of

Explorers. Then switch gears and spend another twenty minutes as if you were all Artists. Then spend twenty minutes as Judges, and finally twenty minutes as Warriors. Be sure to appoint someone to record the learnings from each of these role-playing periods.

How did it help to look at your situation from different vantage points? Was it hard to stay "in role," that is, to not depart from thinking like an Explorer during the first segment, or an Artist in the second, etc.?

3.   Try this exercise with your children. Let them pick the topic. How does their role-playing compare to that of the adults with whom you've worked?

Helpful Resource

• Von Oech, Roger. *A Kick in the Seat of the Pants.* New York: Harper & Row, 1986.

Thinking Hats

You can't solve a problem on the same level it was created. You have to rise above it to the next level.

—ALBERT EINSTEIN

16

Have you ever heard someone say, usually to children, "Let's all put on our thinking caps and imagine this or that"? It's a whimsical invitation to creativity—as if one could become more inventive simply by donning a piece of headgear. Yet Edward de Bono and other researchers have done precisely that by making the fanciful real, using a technique they call "thinking hats" to redirect people's minds and encourage more comprehensive consideration of a given problem, issue, or idea.

In this process, participants "put on" different hats, either imaginary or real. Each hat symbolizes a different perspective on a problem. Whichever hat is being worn at the moment determines the perspective from which everyone discusses the problem at hand.

The hat colors in de Bono's system include *white*, for facts, figures, objective information; *yellow*, for positive aspects of the issue; *black*, for negative aspects of the issue; *green*, for new and creative ideas; *red*, for related emotions and feelings; and *blue*, for control of other hats and the process.[1] Some facilitators create their own hats to suit the problem or add additional perspectives.

The purpose of the thinking-hats strategy, obviously, is to look at a matter from a variety of angles. This vastly enhances understanding. It's essentially a form of gaming, in that it formalizes what happens in the real world anyway—people seeing things differently—but it organizes the varieties of experience in a way that allows each perspective to be heard, honored, and combined with other perspectives, with minimal risk.

"Put On Your Thinking Cap"

Here are four brain teasers to stimulate your creative thinking. Use the strategy of thinking hats to arrive at solutions.

1. Fishermen who had driven two hundred miles to fish in a well-stocked lake were frustrated by high winds sweeping toward the shore. They could not cast out into the teeth of the gale with their light rods. Finally, one man stumbled from the muddy shore with a solution. Can you figure out what it was?

2. During army maneuvers in Canada, it was so cold one morning that only one truck out of about one hundred to be used would start. While several mechanics stood around with hands in pockets, one ingenious individual thought of a way to start the other trucks. What do you think it was?

3. Imagine you are caught in a storm at sea in a powerboat. The boat has lost its rudder. There is nothing aboard by way of an oar or paddle or sail—only a pail to bail out water. How would you steer to harbor?

4. With six wooden matches, make four equilateral triangles. Each match must touch another. No bending or breaking of matches is allowed.

Exercises

1. In a group setting, provide construction paper, color markers, scissors, ribbon, glue, tape, and other craft materials. Divide the group into teams and have each team create one of the six hats described in this chapter.

    When the hats are made, have the group discuss an opportunity or problem with which they are all familiar. To keep the discussion on track, always have someone in the group wearing one of the hats. While that hat is being worn, allow only comments that are focused on the theme represented by that hat (use the color codes indicated in the chapter).

    If someone wants to change the way the group is looking at the subject, he or she needs to wear the appropriate hat.

    As the facilitator, you should wear the blue hat and guide the discussion by intervening at times and asking people to change hats.

    Suggestion: Create a silly hat for use if someone keeps speaking out of turn or breaking the rules. Keep the use of this hat light-hearted, but use it to reinforce the need to keep the discussion focused.

2. Repeat the exercise above, but distribute the hats among six people. The two ground rules of this exercise are that only these six can speak, and each of them must speak or function according to the theme of the hat they are wearing.

3. Try the thinking-hats approach with your children. Consider using it to discuss topics such as these:

    • The family dog is causing problems. What should we do about it?

    • We're running late getting out of the house in the morning. How can we solve that problem?

    • There's a major scheduling problem. How can we solve it?

    • Two siblings are divided over who should get the room of an older sibling who is leaving home. How can you arrive at a decision?

Helpful Resource

- de Bono, Edward. *Six Thinking Hats: The Power of Focused Thinking.* New York: Little, Brown & Co., 1986.

Storyboarding

As Christians, we really do believe that there are other lines of connection than those the world sees, lines which may run in completely different directions. The logic of stories and of lives, then, is not the same as the logic of the logicians.

—**William Kirk Kirkpatrick**

17

As a child, I was told to drink my milk to grow strong bones and teeth. I envisioned the white liquid rushing through my body like a tiny fire truck, with hoses spraying milk anywhere my teeth or bones needed a repair job. It was the ignorance of the amateur who understands nothing of anatomy or physiology, jumping to ridiculous conclusions, oversimplifying, unaware of the parts that make up the healthy functioning of the whole.

Storyboarding—also called compression planning—avoids the dangers of overlooking important components. It carefully sequences the parts in order to produce a unified and efficient whole.

The Origin and Definition of Storyboarding

Storyboarding dates at least to Leonardo da Vinci, perhaps the quintessential creative genius. Leonardo had what he called his "Infinite Wall." Before committing any piece of art to canvas, he would sketch its elements on a wall, as if it were a scratch pad. This first draft approach enabled him to work out the pieces of the work in isolation before drawing them together for a grand and final scheme.

In our own century Walt Disney developed the storyboarding process to the point of near perfection over a forty-five-year period. He credited Leonardo as his inspiration for this approach, as well as his mother, who ran the Disney family from a bulletin board mounted in her kitchen. She had notes, calendars, and reminders affixed in a way that was clear, organized, and highly flexible. Disney used the technique to develop complete motion animation, a breakthrough innovation over the French cartoons of the day, which featured merely speaking characters.

The detail called for in full animation required endless drawings that had to be displayed to determine progress and avoid duplication. *Snow White and the Seven Dwarfs*, for example, required 250,000 drawings in the finished version. Since Disney hated meetings, he devised storyboarding in order to come into the studio and determine at a glance what was completed and what was yet to be done.

"If you can dream it, you can do it."

—Walt Disney, on the creation of Epcot Center

Today advertising agencies, publishers, writers, event planners, and more and more businesses and churches are employing this visual technique. It is not a gimmick but a core strategy for planning. The famed "desktop" used in computer word processing is also a version of storyboarding.

Fundamentally storyboarding is a visual system for developing, displaying, and organizing thoughts, ideas, and plans, using poster boards, cards, or notes affixed to a wall. Webster's Dictionary defines a storyboard as "a panel or series of panels on which is tacked a set of small rough drawings, depicting consecutively the important changes of scene and action in a planned film, television show or act."

Kinds of Storyboards

Disney devised five basic kinds of storyboards for use with any project:

Planning Storyboard

This is an overall guiding device that involves these items:
- A topic card—a 5" x 7" card on which the subject is summarized in a word or two.
- Headers—4" x 6" cards summarizing the main elements of the subject, the first card always being the objective of the project.
- SuBheaders (or "subbers")—3" x 5" cards summarizing subdivisions of each of the headers.
- Siders—half of a 3" x 5" card with peripheral but important issues noted.

Idea Storyboard

This approach is similar to the above, except that each of the headers becomes a topic for an idea storyboard.

Communication Storyboard

This approach looks at the flow of information and who needs to know what, by when, and how.

Organizational Storyboard

This is similar to an organizational chart for a business or organization. It displays operating relationships.

Synapse Storyboard

This involves the bringing together of seemingly unrelated parts into meaningful relationships.

FOUR BASIC STORYBOARDS

PLANNING

IDEAS

COMMUNICATION

ORGANIZATION

The Value of Storyboarding

Storyboarding has at least six advantages.

- It saves time and money. In some groups more ideas are generated in fifteen minutes than have been generated in the previous fifteen months.
- It builds commitment and ownership. People tend to commit to that which they have had a part in discovering and/or shaping.
- Storyboarding provides flexibility. The inherent flexibility of the cards allows for restructuring, reorganizing, or recategorizing at any time. This has a powerful effect on a group, because it facilitates change in a nonthreatening manner. People can see where things fit, and sign off accordingly.
- Storyboarding keeps ideas before the group. A storyboard has great visual value. People aren't just sitting, talking, and taking notes about abstractions. Everyone can see what has been said and agreed on. That helps engender trust. Things are being discussed and decided out in the open, not in a back room somewhere.
- It preserves the results of the process. There's a great "capture" of ideas and energy, and you can leave the results up for a long time.
- It allows people to innovate while participating. Participants can make changes in their thinking and actually see the impact of those changes on the overall discussion. This empowers them to think more broadly and deeply, and to take greater risks conceptually. After all, it's just moving a card on a bulletin board—although actually it's moving the group's thinking into new territory. Low risk, high innovation!

Some Uses for Storyboarding

Storyboarding can be used for long-range planning, for both individuals and institutions; devising a preaching calendar to guarantee a balanced biblical diet for a congregation; sermon preparation (planning a series and individual messages); teaching a course (as a timesaver, this enables one to know what to omit); planning an event, such as an anniversary, a conference, or a dinner; and clarifying the purpose and strategy of a group or committee.

Suggestion: Explore the possibilities of a miniature storyboard by using Post-It notes. Also try storyboarding with a computer.

Exercises

1. Select an area or subject in your organization that needs to be discussed. Pull together a group of people to examine the issue, and facilitate their interaction using a storyboard. Afterwards consider how the storyboard was helpful, and also what you could do to improve its usefulness.

2. Use the storyboard method for one of the following projects:
   - Create an outline for a sermon or Bible study you have to give or a book you'd like to write.
   - Devise an organizational chart for a group with whom you are associated.
   - Evaluate your life story in terms of highlights, low-lights, accomplishments, milestones, hopes, and goals.
   - Chart out the history of your church or organization to show the main events, people, and achievements. Having completed this storyboard, how could you use it to create vision for the future?

Helpful Resource

The McNellis Company, 1100 Eighth Avenue, P.O. Box 582, New Brighton, PA 15066
Tel: 800-569-6015
Fax: 412-847-9275

Barriers to Creativity

The most costly disease in America is neither cancer nor coronaries, but boredom. Transplants are increasingly available—pancreas, kidney, liver, heart, bone marrow, lung—but if a man's mind is devoid of horizons he will succumb to boredom.

—AUTHOR UNKNOWN

18

Wayne Gretzky, the celebrated hockey star, made this observation: "You miss 100 percent of the shots you do not take." The unseen fence around many of us arises from our own reticence to go beyond our self-imposed limits. In our heads we encounter blockage, and for some unanswered reason, we back off.

Why this inhibition? What are the conversational cancer cells that destroy our creative immune system? How easily a few words can kill a good idea! "Killer comments" or "fire-hosing" are the labels we place on negative remarks. See if you can identify with the following:

- "We tried that ten years ago."
- "Let's stick with what works."
- "It's too radical."
- "Great idea, but not for us."
- "We never did that before."
- "We've never done it that way before."
- "Be practical."
- "That won't work here."

- "It will be more trouble than it's worth."
- "People will never buy it."

Comments such as these bury an idea before considering its merits. When your initial reaction to a new idea is negative, think before you speak. Don't erase the idea from your mind. Try to see something positive. Often a new idea has a long way to go. Anyone willing to improve and/or develop an idea deserves support. So instead of throwing ice water on someone's enthusiasm, offer encouragement, expertise, and constructive suggestions.

Try some creative "fertilizers," such as these:

- "That's a great idea. See if you can develop it!"
- "That sounds interesting. Tell me more."
- "I never thought of that. Let's explore your suggestions."
- "You may be on to something. That's the kind of thinking we celebrate."

Better yet, help the creative spirits in your group think through their ideas. Stretch their thinking by asking these or other questions:

- "What makes that interesting to you?"
- "Have you thought about how we might handle the follow-through?"
- "What would be your next step?"
- "You might get some good help on that from people out in the field."
- "Could you be prepared to bring that before our board?"

For fear of ridicule, we tend to play the game too safely. We commonly bring forth ideas only when we are sure of their worth and acceptance. But creative minds often need encouragement.

**"Obstacles are the frightful things you see
when you take your eyes off of the goal."**

—Byrd Baggett

Who are the chief culprits who discourage creative thinkers? Most of us have encountered them. One group is parents. Another is cultural phenomena. Then there are teachers, and of course television. And the final coffin nail is the aging process—usually self-driven. Let's consider these in turn.

Parents

Too frequently, parents blurt out, "Don't do that!" or "Why are you always asking so many dumb questions?" or "You can't do anything right!" or the particularly poisonous "You'll never amount to anything!"

Isador Rabi, Nobel Prize winner, was interviewed after receiving his award. A journalist asked him, "How did you become a scientist?" He responded, "My mother." "Oh, was she a scientist?" "No, but every day when I came home from school, she would ask, 'So, did you ask any intelligent questions today?'"

"That," he ventured, "is the genius of a good scientist."

Parents who answer questions with labels and are too busy to cultivate their children's curiosity seldom read to their children or know how to play. They do not understand that a child's toys are his tools for learning. Thus these unresponsive parents tend to squelch the natural tendency all children have to express creativity.

Years ago I taught a seminary student who was uncommonly gifted. He had graduated from an Ivy League school, and his transcript record indicated an I.Q. of 160. He also came highly recommended by the evangelical community. One of his university referees, head of a science department for more than thirty years, wrote, "Never before have I had a student in this young man's league. I'm sorry he is going to waste his life by going into the ministry."

Not long after enrolling, this same young man stood at my desk, telling me, as I listened incredulously, that he was leaving. "I'm checking it to you, Prof. I don't think I have what it takes for the ministry."

"Why?" I insisted. I thought to myself, "I'd better not tell anyone else around here that *this* guy doesn't have it, or they'll *all* be heading for the registrar's office to resign!"

"Let me ask you a few questions," I said to him. "Tell me about your family." "It's a disaster," he replied. "Tell me about your father," I prodded. "That's worse. I would come home from school with a 98 on an exam—the highest grade in the class—and he would ask, 'Where are the other two points?' His favorite name for me was 'Dummy.'"

Have you ever been called "Dummy" by the most significant person in your life, even though you had exceptionally high intelligence, and had graduated with honors from a premier university? It didn't matter that everyone else encouraged this fellow. He believed his father. This is tragic testimony to the fact that parents are capable of serving as the most significant morticians.

Teachers

In both public and private schools, as well as in Sunday schools, teachers abound who declare, "We don't ask those questions here." When I hear that sort of warning, I think, "If not, why not? Where will a child secure adequate answers to crucial questions?"

While conducting a class on communication, I assigned the students a personal project: Come to class with a creative presentation of Acts 3:1–10.

The next class hour was alive with a potpourri of creative genius. There were dramas, songs with fresh lyrics, paintings, cartoons, videos, and many other approaches. But one of the finest pieces of work was a free verse poem. I had never heard anything like it. The student was reluctant to read it at first, having been divested of his confidence by a previous instructor. But when he finally summoned the courage to read his composition to the class, he was met with thunderous applause—even a standing ovation! In fact, it took several minutes to restore order.

Tears were streaming from his eyes. So I asked him, "Have you ever done anything like this before?"

"Only in private," he said softly. "How come?" I asked. And then he poured out a tear-jerking story.

He told the class that a fifth-grade teacher had asked the students to come to class with a model of their home in cardboard. He had worked feverishly on the project. But when he brought his model up to the teacher's desk, he got the shock of his life.

"She took one look at my work and said, 'That's the dumbest thing I've ever seen,' then crushed it in her hands, throwing it in the wastebasket next to her desk. So, Prof," the student continued, finishing his story, "I never ran that risk again. Then you asked us to come up with a creative project, and I thought I would give it one more chance. I believed you and decided to go for broke."

If you think that student is an exception, you are out of touch with reality. After almost fifty years of graduate teaching, I have discovered that one of my primary tasks is to convince students that I believe in them—even when others do not. In fact, they don't even believe in themselves.

Never forget: The act of teaching is the act of awakening the natural curiosity and abilities of young, plastic minds.

Eight Principles for Learning

1. Learning is fundamentally social.
2. Cracking the whip stifles learning.
3. Learning needs an environment that supports it.
4. Learning crosses hierarchical bounds.
5. Self-directed learning fuels the fire.
6. Learning by doing is more powerful than memorizing.
7. Failure to learn is often the fault of the system, not the people.
8. Sometimes the best learning is unlearning.

—*Brigitte Jordan,* Fast Company, *special edition, 1996*

Television

"In American society, TV is the generator of reality," Robert Hughes informs us. Long before many children learn to read, they discover how to turn on a television set. As a result, their young minds absorb the deadening nuances of our secular, nihilistic society.

The old maxim applies: "Garbage in; garbage out." This beast out of the sea is arguably the greatest ingenuity killer of all. Neil Postman's landmark study of the entertainment culture, *Amusing Ourselves to Death*, concludes with "The Huxleyan Warning," in which he says, "There are two ways by which the spirit of a culture may be shriveled. In the first—the Orwellian—culture becomes a prison. In the second—the Huxleyan—culture becomes a burlesque."[1]

Postman then suggests that Huxley's *Brave New World* offers one of our century's most powerful metaphors about the destruction of personal and social freedom—a world in which people come to *love* the technologies that take away their capacity to think, destroy their critical faculties, and deprive them of their autonomy, maturity, and history. Is it possible that Huxley's prediction is coming true?

People conditioned by mindless violence, mayhem, and perverted sex can hardly be expected to form the cheering section for creative potential.

As a result of excessive and unmonitored exposure to this plug-in drug of choice, we are now harvesting tragic results: people who can no longer read, write, think, or *become creative.* Passivity, dependence, and boredom are the diseases with which we are infected. Our generation has embraced the McDonald's slogan: "We do it all for you." Soft societies do not produce great leaders—or creative thinkers.

On the other hand television can be a teaching tool, a stimulus to meaningful discussion, and a primer for the study of language, history, and economics. If we refuse to become its slave and make it an adjunct instructor, television can be a remarkable aid to creativity.

The Aging Process

When a person grows old enough to remember the days when driving on two-lane roads was the order of the day, he or she often grows weary of newfangled inventions. For such elders, the wind in their sails has died down. Dreaming and remembering often overtake planning and expectations. Why do some people decline as they grow older, while others become more vigorous and manage to respond and adjust to changes? How can the resources of elderly folks be tapped?

> "Dr. Ashley Montagu once wrote that your goal in life should be to die young—as late as possible. The most creative people I know live by that maxim. They are as curious, engaged, and innocent as children. They keep asking questions, wrestling with interesting problems, looking at the world through an ever-changing lens."
>
> —*Michael Csikszentmihalyi, quoted in Anna Muoio, ed., 'They Have a Better Idea . . . Do You?"* Fast Company *(August/September 1997): 73.*

It is important to understand that older people do not normally do what young people do. Instead, they instinctively apply their experience from years of active life, when bodily strength and agility peaked, to an important component of creativity—*wisdom*. The Hebrew word for wisdom means "skill in living life well." What better group to enhance creative planning than senior citizens?

When combined with the exuberance of youth, the prudence of old age can enrich a group immeasurably. Cicero asked, "For what is more charming than old age surrounded by the enthusiasm of youth?" We do our ministries a great disservice when we exclude mature minds, isolating them and allowing them to disappear. The tragedy of life is not in the fact of death but in what dies inside us while we live.

"Retirement," observed Norman Cousins, which is "supposed to be a chance to join the winner's circle, has turned out to be more dangerous than automobiles or LSD . . . a chance to do everything that leads to nothing. It is the gleaming brass ring that unhorses the rider."[2]

America's aging population requires a twofold involvement from its Christian ministries. First, the creative use of mature thinking in everyday affairs provides a needed additive to many ministry problems. Think tanks need gray heads.

Second, innovative solutions are needed for the four-part dilemma of old age: income, health, living arrangements, and life purpose. This quartet of needs is highlighted by John W. Gardner, with a plea to give people, before retirement, "the kinds of experience that will build the capacity for self-renewal."[3]

Gardner concedes that we have made substantial progress in the first three aging concerns. But the least recognized and most neglected is the last, life purpose. This one is at the heart of the creative process. One of the reasons mature people stop learning is that they become less and less willing to risk failure. We need to help them to win.[4]

Of course, Scripture speaks about these needs. Psalm 78:5–6 underscores intergenerational dependence: "He commanded our forefathers to teach their children, so the next generation would know them [i.e., 'the praiseworthy deeds of the Lord, his power, and the wonders he has done' v. 4]—even the children yet to be born, and they in turn would tell their children."

Seniors need to be needed. But in turn, young people need them as well. This advancing army of seasoned life veterans remains largely an untapped resource for many Christian ministries. The goal should be: every active mind a reproducing cell of creative thought.

"The thing is to become a master and in your old age to acquire the courage to do what children did when they knew nothing."

—Henry Miller

The barrier of advancing age can easily be counterbalanced. Consider these ministry methods:
- use of the telephone to survey opinions of older people
- use of computers by older folks unable to travel
- solicitation of written materials from seniors
- oral histories to enrich a body of believers
- pairing of old and young for birthdays or other celebrations
- sharing or trading off skills to supply medical needs

"Responsibility for learning and growth rests finally with the individual. We can reshape the environment to remove obstacles. We can stimulate and challenge. But in the last analysis the individual must foster his own development. At any age, the chief resource must be the individual's own interest, drive and enthusiasm."[5]

Exercises

1. How would you say your parents helped or hindered your creativity? In light of your answers to this question, what practical things can you do to encourage—and not discourage—your own children's or grandchildren's creative possibilities?

2. Name one teacher whom you remember as particularly effective at helping you learn. What was it about this person that caused you to embrace the subject or skill he or she was teaching?

3. Here's a real challenge! Unplug the TV in your house for one full week. If you can last that long, ask yourself the following questions at the end of that period:
    - What happened after the TV was gone?
    - How did we feel when we realized that TV was no longer an option for our time?
    - What did we do with the time created by not having the TV to watch?
    - What new things (if any) did we do or try?
    - In what ways does not having a TV force us to be creative in how we spend our time?

4. Arrange to pay a visit to some individuals in their 80s or 90s. Ask permission ahead of time to "interview" them on their recollections of life during the early part of this century as compared to today. Ask them about their own stories, and their impressions about such things as the development of the telephone system, baseball, D-Day, penicillin, the Work Projects Administration (WPA), radio programs, and the interstate highway system.

    What are their opinions of life today? What advice would they give young people just starting out? What was the most significant event in their lifetime? What do they think the world will be like in the future?

Helpful Resources

- Postman, Neil. *Amusing Ourselves to Death*. New York: Viking-Penguin, 1985.
- vonOech, Roger. *A Whack on the Side of the Head*. New York: Warner Books, 1983.

Creativity and Your Family

Every day you should be seeing the world in a new and personal way. The tree outside your house is no longer the same—so look at it. Your husband, wife, child, mother, father all are changing daily, so look at them. Everything is in the process of change, including you.

—LEO BUSCAGLIA

19

Home is where the heart is, they say. Quips and jokes about the home abound: It's where you can take off your new shoes and put on your old manners. It's where people go when they get tired of being nice to people. Yet however lightly we regard it, the home is the nest from which we all take flight, and one of the most influential factors in our creativity is the quality of our home life.

This fact has profound implications. As Glenn Stanton put it, "The face of family life in America has undergone a radical transformation. We have become a nation of family relativists, with no clear and common idea of what family relationships ought to look like . . . no common script for family life . . . accustomed to allowing the players to cast their own roles, and write their own lines according to their personal desires. . . . Radical autonomy is now our defining virtue."[1]

At first glance this footloose, fancy-free lifestyle may look like a good recipe for creativity: "Do your own thing!" Wrong! Creativity arises from a sense of security, from freedom within boundaries that define personhood and community welfare. A child cannot become a person of worth without early guidance in the discovery process.

How Can We Produce Creative Families?

In her classic text *The Magic Years* Selma Fraiberg explained that all babies work indefatigably on discovery. Infants fall in love with the world they have discovered through their mothers' love.[2] But the principle of pure pleasure and the imaginary world the child sees must be educated to oppose magic thinking. That job, asserted Fraiberg, "demands the greatest intuitive knowledge and skill on the part of the parents."[3]

If mother and father do not have their marriage on an even keel, this important preparation of imagination can be severely handicapped. The quality of the marriage determines the quality of the family. Thus creative couples tend to produce creative children.

Creative people are most frequently the products of warm, communal families that allow mutual participation in a host of different activities. Children enter the world with healthy curiosity but can quickly become noncreative if the significant persons conditioning their environment—their parents or guardians—prove dysfunctional.

Three groups welded together make an invincible combination for lasting character training. But note who has the child most often:

- The church has 1 percent of the child's time.
- The school has 18 percent of the child's time.
- The home has 81 percent of the child's time.

These proportions lay a heavy responsibility on parents as the primary developers of their children's potential. They will have the most determinative influence. Even with all the demands of work and other commitments outside the home, parents can make home a safe, nurturing environment, where creative achievements are celebrated as a high priority.

However, let's not overlook the significant role the church needs to play. Granted, a local church has relatively limited time with a child, but it needs to make the most of the time it does have. That's why church leaders need to commit themselves to authentic Christian education.

Too often, the Sunday-school hour is viewed as a throwaway—a glorified form of babysitting while the adults attend their worship service. What a tragedy! Besides being terribly uncreative, that is highly irresponsible. That mind-set reflects a defeatist attitude: "We only have an hour or so, and what can you really accomplish in an hour?" The answer: plenty, *if* you use it creatively!

For proof, we have only to turn on the TV, where the average children's program runs no more than an hour, and many are only half that long. Yet some, like "Sesame Street" or "Wishbone," are legendary in their ability to engage children's minds. Obviously, the average church has nowhere near the resources to devote to their Sunday-school program as are needed to create TV shows. But the point is not money but the intention to do something worthwhile with every minute a young person spends at church.

I'm reminded of the motto of Jim Rayburn, founder of Young Life: "It's a sin to bore a kid with the gospel." So what is your church doing with the 1 percent it has of a child's time?

The other institution that needs to support parents in their developmental task is the school. Unfortunately schools as they are currently configured may or may not contribute much to a child's creative development. Concerning our schools, John Gardner has written: "The pieces of the educational revolution are lying around unassembled. Education needs more than dollars. We are not going to succeed in solving the major problems facing us, without substantial innovation."[4]

Much could be said about the potential and prospects for such innovation. But I want to devote this chapter to what families can do to foster creativity. Let's consider four arenas for engagement of the creative process.

Modeling

Professor Albert Bandura of Stanford University has called modeling the greatest form of unconscious learning. The pattern demonstrated by a parent, grandparent, aunt, uncle, or other significant adult who consistently thinks and acts with a zest for living can make a deep and lasting impression on a child.

Unfortunately just about the time a child becomes most receptive to such modeling, many parents go through a midlife crisis in which they plateau. Their lives become stale, and they suffer from a severe case of the blahs. The spirit hardens, and the mind runs to the safety of the familiar.

My wife remembers her own distaste as a child for some of the women in her church who always sat in the same seats, wore the same hats, talked to the same people, and said the same things Sunday after Sunday after Sunday. It was improper to say it out loud then, but today's child would accurately summarize that monotonous scene with one word: "Booooooooooring!"

Your home should never be boring. Not that you have to entertain your children twenty-four hours a day; entertainment is not the same as creativity. No, I'm suggesting that your home become a mini-foundry where young minds are shaped by the intensity of hot ideas, fervent gamesmanship, and energetic activity. What a child experiences in those early stretching years will largely determine his level of adult creativity. Therefore we parents and grandparents constantly need to shake ourselves awake (1 Cor. 11:1; Phil. 4:9; Eph. 5:14). The operative word is *motivation.*

Stimulation in the home often comes through a family's participation in special celebrations. While visiting the Wailing Wall in Jerusalem, I witnessed three Bar Mitzvah ceremonies. The festivities included the boys sitting on the shoulders of their fathers, uncles, and friends as they danced to traditional music. Women threw candy to them, and there was great jubilation. As I witnessed this site, I thought to myself, "These young men will never forget this moment!"

In my hometown of Dallas, a Protestant church observes a solemn rite of passage for thirteen-year-old boys called the "march to manhood." During a special Sunday service, the minister asks each boy two questions: "Are you ready to accept the challenge that you are about to take, to accept the responsibility of being a man? If so, say, 'I am.'

"Are you ready to uphold the family name, and to carry yourself in a manner that will be pleasing to God, yourself, and your community? If so, say, 'I am.'"

Let me tell you, when that young man, standing before his family, the friends of his family, his peers, his youth leaders, and the other members of his church community, responds with the words, "I am," the ritual anchors him to his roots and serves to prod his thinking and order his priorities.

Rituals like these have biblical precedent in Deuteronomy 6:6–9: "These commandments that I give you today are to be upon your hearts. Impress them on your children. Talk about them when you sit at home and when you walk along the road, when you lie down and when you get up. Tie them as symbols on your hands and bind them on your foreheads. Write them on the doorframes of your house and your gates." Truth is more caught than taught.

Surroundings

If we think of ourselves as Shakespeare described us—actors playing our roles in life's drama—we arrive as free spirits, surrounded by a variety of stimulating props to make life come alive. As children, we eagerly respond. If we are nurtured against a backdrop that encourages curiosity and wonder, the whole world becomes a classroom. Creativity is not just an instrument; it is an environment.

A family friend who had taught biology before she had children turned every crawling bug or insect into a subject for study for her curious youngsters. Every plant or animal, every storm or night sky, was likely to be discussed. As a result, her children have grown up to be fascinating (and fascinated) people with boundless mental energies.

Every home needs a "creative living center," perhaps a family room, crammed with resources such as these:

- A slide and/or film projector and screen, tape recorder, and VCR. The key is to teach children *how* to use these aids to learning. Make them family property and use them to stimulate visual creativity, dramatic possibilities, and the art of telling a story.

- A chalkboard and/or magnetic whiteboard, bulletin board, and storyboard, with appropriate chalk, markers, magnets, tacks, etc.— all invitations to imaginative thinking and planning.

- Books, magazines (especially used ones), newspapers, booklets, pamphlets, and the like (carefully chosen, of course, for appropriate content).

- An abundance of basic tools, such as scissors, paper, paste, crayons, chalk, and the like. As children grow older, tools for more difficult tasks need to be available, such as those for building models, musical instruments, a globe, a telescope, a microscope—whatever aids their inquisitive minds.

- A computer, which opens an even wider world—but only if it is a means to an end, not an end in itself.

Whenever possible, make things instead of buying them. One of my enjoyable experiences was constructing a doll house for my grandchildren and adding to it each year.

Creativity thrives in an environment devoid of crutches but invaded by fully alive people—friends, neighbors, fellow-workers, a cross-section of the community. Every family should be involved in some service-oriented ministry project, often crossing cultural barriers. Young people are energized by a torrential drive to be useful. Perhaps this may be fulfilled through babysitting or chores for the elderly or disabled.

Children learn from crossing traditional boundaries. If possible, young people should visit outside their own country. On one occasion, our family spent a Christmas vacation visiting missionaries in Mexico. The experience yielded untold benefits, as well as pleasure and lots of memories to add to our scrapbook. If your family lives in a rural setting, you should make a habit of taking your kids to the city. Conversely, an urban family can only benefit by visiting the country.

Many families seem to look good from a distance, but they are not really healthy. The toxic shock to family health is self-centeredness. Thus family celebrations should incorporate not only something new—a different way to wrap packages, a twist on old traditions, a touch of creative humor—but a sharing of selves with each other.

One of the wealthiest but most generous men I have ever known grew up in a home where everything a child could want was readily available. I asked him on one occasion how he had avoided becoming materialistic. He revealed the secret of his wise use of money by replying, "My parents taught us that everything we owned was either a tool to be used or an idol to be worshiped." What a valuable perspective for all of us!

Playtime

If you want to develop creativity in your home, place a high premium on children's toys. Toys are the tools they will use for creative learning. Here are some principles for selecting toys:

- Don't emphasize quantity as much as quality. What matters is not how many toys your child has but what kind. Your children's toys should foster physical dexterity, mental challenge, esthetic growth, and social development.
- Use everyday objects whenever possible. Boxes, cans, pieces of wood (all examined for safety), and a variety of packing and promotional materials can be recycled for productive playtime. At Christmas the boxes may be a bigger hit for a small child than the contents.
- Choose toys that encourage children to be creative. One of the best options is puppets, possibly handmade. Everyone in the family can be involved in building the stage, creating the scripts, designing the costumes, and performing the sketches.
- Do not use toys as a substitute for personal time and individual involvement. We have all heard the poignant story of a little child asking Santa Claus for a mommy or a daddy. Every child has a paramount need for loving personal attention.

Family Togetherness

Certain areas of family life can become stagnant and unattractive to children unless creative ideas are used. Here are some categories to consider:
- *Family worship.* This often becomes boring, predictable, and parent-centered. Instead, allow your children to help plan and participate.
- *Family recreation.* This needs to be more than good intentions. It needs to be scheduled activities, geared to age requirements. Toddlers need recreation that is varied in small blocks of time. Teens, preparing for adulthood, require larger time frames and must assume some responsibility in planning and implementation. Teens especially tend to thrive on competition and challenges.
- *Family hospitality.* The use of the home for evangelism or Christian growth groups provides abundant opportunity for children to see God at work. Age, race, culture, occupation, and economic diversity all combine to stimulate a child's outlook on real life.

- *Special occasions.* Birthdays, anniversaries, graduations, and other milestones are ideal opportunities to learn how to honor another person. Each member of the family can have a part in planning and executing the menus, decorations, and presents, along with special poems, music, or drama. A child needs to learn that although life is not a merry-go-round of nonstop fun, there can be an aspect of merriment to almost every experience.

- *Travel.* New places, new people, and new activities always stir a child's curiosity. Whenever possible, take the family or part of it on ministry trips. Allow them to see their mother or father in a professional role. Help them understand the principle of adapting to other people's requirements. Seek opportunities to travel to new and historical places. Plan mystery trips, and give each family member a responsibility to make it a memorable success.

- *Tabletime.* Tables tend toward togetherness. Use yours not only for eating meals but for games, discussion, planning, reading, and praying. My wife's first experience of family worship occurred at the breakfast table after she had spent the night at a friend's house. It helped to lay a foundation for her own motherhood in later years. Ideally everyone should take part in table talk. Invite others to join you, especially those whose cultures may be unfamiliar. For example, foreign exchange students greatly enrich a family.

- *Finances.* Money plays a major role in our contemporary world. Therefore families need to pray, study, discuss, and plan projects for every child to learn to use money creatively.[5]

- *Husband-wife relationship.* Children, the Scriptures teach, are arrows to be launched into the world (Ps. 127:4). Mother and father continue as a love unit whether or not children are present. The number-one enemy of happy marriages is not money, adultery, or incompatibility but boredom! Creativity is essential to keep a love relationship polished.

A balance between planned activities that are structured and those that allow free expression furnish a growing space for spontaneity.

ALONE TIME	PEOPLE TIME
WORK TIME	PLAY TIME

Which of these four areas is most difficult for you? Why? What can be done to make them more contributory to your family's creative development?

What will our children remember from their family life? The wisdom of Proverbs reminds us, "A cheerful heart is good medicine, but a crushed spirit dries up the bones" (Prov. 17:22). Creative activity produces an overflow of endorphins, a source of one's own cortisone.

Families fail when the people in them stagnate. They come alive when the members of the family enliven their dormant creative genius. Good parents provide both roots and wings. Roots instill character—gratitude, honesty, trustworthiness. Wings lift those traits to unimaginable heights with creative updrafts that benefit everyone and reproduce the aliveness that Jesus Christ came to give us.

How Can We Correct a Noncreative Lifestyle?

Recent research on family life in America indicates that many families, both Christian and non-Christian, exist in a tiresome daily routine with little variation. Exhausted parents and colorless children grind out days on end in trite and uneventful lives. Sooner or later, some of these folks show up in Christian ministries, often hoping to find a spark of something to diversify their lives.

Good news awaits them: Creativity can be learned. It can be installed in a home where innovative thinking has not been the pattern before. Let's consider four components of the reversal process.

Evaluation

In his classic primer on home life, *Values Begin at Home*, Ted Ward notes that families are caught between two forces: first, the strong, self-sufficient, independent family, and second, the institutionalism that presses hard in every community.[6]

Family basics are universal, God-given, and reconfirmed in every generation. But developing a creative family—or restoring a noncreative family to creativity—must begin with the recognition that the family itself is a value to be honored within the culture where it exists. A healthy, creative family always builds on fidelity and responsibility as an evidence of love for each other.

From this starting point, any family can build a creative lifestyle. Parents, of course, must set the pace through a willingness to communicate and the courage to be honest. If redirection is to succeed, the status quo must be reexamined. What are the areas slated for change?

Ideally a "family council" should be convened. Everyone of school age and over should be gathered for a discussion in which all need to participate. All ideas should be put on the table. This calls for a brainstorming session (see chapter 9). Obviously mutual respect and good manners are vital as a starting point. The odds of such a meeting being productive are high if it is conducted properly. Everyone wants improvement, because families meet deep personal needs. The entire experience should be positive and upbeat, with humor and good will.

Teamwork

Liberated spirits foster creative lifestyles. If a family truly wants to initiate a fresh mode of daily home life, it must adopt a help-each-other mindset. When children can be assured that their parents are people of their word and are firmly supportive of the children's ideas, when parents can count on their children to obey the rules, then the emotional air in the home is cleared for creative ideas to flourish.

Teamwork rests solidly on adherence to a few underlying rules in the context of loving leadership. Ward prompts our thinking about how a sense of right and wrong emerges in children. To know the difference, he says, is part of a child's survival.[7] But it has limitations, as the apostle Paul noted in 1 Corinthians 13:11: "When I was a child, I spoke . . . thought . . . reasoned as a child."

A "child's" viewpoint, in the context of 1 Corinthians 13, is a self-centered universe with self-satisfying values. The child sees other people as "things" and morality as determined by rewards and punishments. Everything is interpreted in light of how it affects his life, and he must keep testing the limits to find out what the rules *really* are. These matters become all-important for parents who seek to reverse an unimaginative home life into a creative one.

Goal-Setting

Having measured the family and established a foundational team spirit, the next step is to make family objectives clear. What do we want to do? A most helpful chapter on this subject is included by Eric Buehrer, former inner-city schoolteacher, in his book *Charting Your Family's Course*. His "navigational principle": Self-management is the key to navigating anything. The challenge of setting goals for a child combines three elements: ability + desire + effort = achievement.[8]

Remember, however, that the Christian family must always maintain a dynamic balance between God's sovereign control over life and our own management. We tend to slide to extremes, either becoming passive—expecting God to do great things without our effort—or grabbing the reins ourselves, yet expecting God to bless our efforts.

"Successful people in any field are those who make a habit of doing the things that failures don't want to do. Persistent pursuit of goals leads to success."[9]

Three rudimentary principles must rule this process:

Any goal you set must be realistic. Unrealistic goals are those without enough time or resources to accomplish them. Also create the desire to accomplish them.

Define goals specifically. General "want-to's" rarely get finished, so be specific.

Break down goals into specific small steps. This principle is particularly important for young children, but it applies to all. Success breeds success.

Affirmation

The most important commandment, Jesus said, is to love the Lord our God with all our hearts (Matt. 22:37). We humans cannot ultimately define or practice love as He commanded unless we imitate Him. "This is love: not that we loved God, but that he loved us, and sent his son as an atoning sacrifice for our sins" (1 John 4:10). God gave us the pattern; every believing parent has a built-in measurement by which to judge how to love a child.

John also wrote, "How great is the love the Father lavished on us, that we should be called children of God" (3:1). Imperfect though we (and our children) may be, acceptance and motivating love flows from the Father. This strong personal support is the motivating factor for creativity in a child. He or she wants desperately to please mom and dad. If the child understands the ethos of his family; if the behavioral guidelines are in place; and if the child knows that the family rule book allows exploration and experimentation, then without fear of rejection natural inquisitiveness will result in creative behavior.

Our twelve-year-old granddaughter, who lives in a loving, supportive family, "needed" money for a hobby goal. She was free to do anything within the family's general understanding of behavior. Her bright idea centered on her love of writing. She, with the help of her sister and her dad's old computer, now at home, created a neighborhood newspaper during summer vacation. House pets, door knockers, landscaping, and unusual collections of neighbors were among the "stories" they covered, as well as pros and cons on controversial community and school issues.

But who would pay for such a sheet? They visited local stores and ran stories on their operations, and also sold them advertising for a fee. They sold copies door-to-door for a few cents each, and by the end of the summer, they had netted several hundred dollars—more than enough to meet the twelve-year-old's goal.

Family boundaries can be greatly enlarged, and every expansion represents an opportunity to let a dry and withering world see Jesus Christ at work in a family.

Exercises

1. Take your family on a mini-vacation in town. Plan a long weekend in which every family member can participate. Explore the historical, geological, and/or cultural resources within fifty miles

of your home. End the weekend with a special favorite meal.

2. Create a "family theater" or skit night. This could be a regular event, conceived, written, and staged by the children with the parents (and maybe extended family and neighbors) as the audience.

3. Plant flowers and vegetables as a family competition. Offer a special reward for the best product.

4. Keep a family journal. Allow each member to write a "state of the family" page at an appointed time of the year, such as at the end of school or at Christmas.

5. Team up with a neighbor family and have an "open house" or reception to honor a teacher, a retiring crossing guard, a coach, or some other person who is important to the neighborhood children.

6. Watch a TV program in which everyone in the family can take an interest, and afterward hold a family discussion.

7. Use competition for special privileges: for example, who can find the most interesting three-minute story from the encyclopedia to tell at the dinner table?

8. Make scrapbooks to commemorate special events.

9. Plan a game day (you may want to plan this and then keep it in reserve for a wet, cold, or snowy day indoors).

10. Make family members "specialists" in certain chores: for example, window washers, brass polishers, drawer organizers, clippers of coupons or news articles, bow-tie experts for packages, table arrangers, pet groomers, etc.

Helpful Resources

- Arp, David, and Claudia Arp. *Ten Great Dates to Revitalize Your Marriage.* Grand Rapids: Zondervan, 1997.
- Blue, Ron, and Judy Blue. *Raising Money-Smart Kids.* Nashville: Thomas Nelson, 1992.
- Buehrer, Eric. *Charting Your Family's Course.* Wheaton, Ill.: Victor Books, 1994.
- LeFever, Marlene D. *Growing Creative Children.* Elgin, Ill.: David C. Cook , 1981.

- Lewis, Robert. *Family Values*. Gresham, Oreg.: Vision House, 1995.
- Swindoll, Charles R. *The Strong Family*. Portland, Oreg.: Multnomah, 1990.
- Ward, Ted. *Values Begin at Home*. Wheaton, Ill.: Victor Books, 1979.
- Wyrtzen, David. *Raising Worldly-Wise but Innocent Kids*. Chicago: Moody, 1990.

Creativity and
the Ministry

*The world is protean: Each generation has the
world to deal with in a new form.*

—EUGENE PETERSON

"A walloping great congregation is fine and fun," observed Martin
Thornton, "but what most communities really need is a couple of saints.
The tragedy is that they may well be there in embryo, waiting to be discovered, waiting for sound training, waiting to be emancipated from the
cult of the mediocre."[1]

Ministry has never been more demanding or more determinative than
it is today, on the cusp of the twenty-first century. The question persists:
How can we extricate our people from the mania of mediocrity? The
Christian community in the Western world needs a larger corps of leaders who model creativity in every aspect of service for the Savior.

This chapter is designed to invade ten critical areas of ministry. It does
not try to provide all the answers but to provoke thinking and to reason a
bit differently and with a creative perspective. If we can get believers to
butcher some of their sacred cows, there is no limit to the possibilities for
significant change.

Communication

Nowhere is communication more critical than in sharing God's message with society. Failure here is eternal in its consequences. It is certainly not admirable to clothe the truth of God with rags, diminishing its glory.

"The way the gospel is conveyed," observed Eugene Peterson, "is as much a part of the kingdom as the truth presented. Why are pastors experts on the truth and dropouts on the way?"[2]

Evangelicals tend to be long on revelation and short on relevance. "The gospel must be preached afresh and told in new ways to every generation," said Helmut Thielicke, "since every generation has its own unique questions. The gospel must constantly be forwarded to a new address, because the recipient is repeatedly changing his place of residence."[3]

In a personal conversation John Stott observed, "It's not too difficult to be biblical if you don't care about being relevant. And it's not too difficult to be relevant if you don't care about being biblical. But to be both biblical and relevant is the art of expository preaching."[4] The creative process seeks to make things relevant.

Are our user-friendly churches being used? Are we dangerously infected with the consumerism of our age? A layperson said it so well: "I don't mind the preacher scratching my back for me, but I do mind him telling me where I itch."

The tyranny of the ordinary holds many Christian ministries hostage. Conservative beliefs can easily be distorted and misused, while stability, prevention, and restraint are used as excuses for opposition to innovation and progressive fortitude. The twin structural supports for a vibrant ministry are clear: authentic biblical teaching paired with fresh, enriching, and relevant functions.

The commercial world calls the welding of clear message with effective methods "communications art," defined by Henry Beer, world-famous designer of shopping malls, as "connecting our clients to their audience."[5]

If the contemporary church desires constant connectedness, it will require a new coat of paint on a regular basis. "Christian organizations are a monument to a great work of God in another generation," said John Warwick Montgomery. We need to give greater attention to both our content (the *what*) and our form (the *how*). People today are asking hard questions and demanding substantive answers. Perhaps that's why Lewis Sperry Chafer observed that "the art of preaching the gospel is the art of saying the same thing over and over again in different ways."

I once saw a fascinating ad: "We could not improve our product so we improved the box." Not a bad suggestion for the gospel. Let's not tamper with the message, but let's vary the packaging.

Some Practical Suggestions

A greater use of drama. The theatrical arts can be employed either to create a need or to summarize, in terms of application. The possibilities are limitless.

A more extensive use of multimedia (slides, overheads, video, and film clips). More media enhances the visual impact. But be sure to monitor technical details. Nothing will ruin the message more than a faulty mechanical production.

A well-devised panel—in effect, representatives who speak for the listeners. One time when I was preaching in an evening service in a West Coast church, the pastor informed me just as we were about to start, "After your message there will be a panel of five people who will be plying you with questions. I'm sure you won't mind."

I thought, "*Now* he informs me!" On the panel were a housewife, a plumber, a teenager, a returned missionary, and a truck driver. They were a sharp group of inquirers, and what a profitable evening that turned out to be. In fact, I was there long past dismissal time discussing pertinent issues. The panel opened up a way for me to get into the real issues this congregation wanted to explore.

Questions and answers. Individual needs are met when participants feel free to ask questions. Since Socrates, we have known that a provocative question is the shortest distance between two philosophical points. The strategy is hardly innovative, but it is one of the most effective. Obviously this format, along with any other that is unfamiliar to the church, needs to be introduced gradually. But an honest query invariably guarantees an energized response.

One word of caution: Question-and-answer sessions are most helpful in a tension-free atmosphere. You can disarm an audience with humor and with total authenticity.

If we ultimately fail as an evangelical community, it will not be because we used the wrong medium but because we did not communicate the right message. Carl Henry astutely observed, "Many Christians now live among neighbors who, swept by tides of immorality, fear herpes more than they fear Hades, and some even think God is a lofty synonym for gobbledygook."[6]

No man ever communicated more effectively than Jesus Christ. What He said and what He did were always perfectly congruent. Effective news reporting—and that is what we are about: reporting *good* news—must back up the message with the life. Walter Wink affirms, "The contagion of holiness overcomes the contagion of uncleanness."

People are often repelled by Christians but irresistibly drawn to Jesus Christ. As Philip Yancey lamented, "Many, far too many, abandon the quest entirely; repelled by the church, they never make it to Jesus."[7]

Governance

Behind the scenes, creativity is as important—or even more so—than on the public platform. The work crews of decision-makers determine what happens in any ministry. An illustration from the business world comes to mind.

While staying at one of the most smoothly operating and efficient hotels I have ever experienced, I had the pleasure of accompanying the CEO through a "back-of-the-house" tour. It was a guided visit to each department, unannounced. As we visited the laundry, the kitchens, the security center, and other areas, the executive not only asked questions about how the department functioned, but invited comments. Any mystery about why the facility was successful became obvious. These people were in the right places for them and they liked what they were doing. They took ownership of their jobs. No wonder this company, out of thirty-four thousand applicants, received the coveted Baldridge Award!

Let's apply this to the church and ministry organizations. There are

4.5 million boards in America, including nonprofit organizations. Tragically, boards of all kinds continue to be trapped in an inadequate design for their jobs and in a destructive set of sloppy habit patterns. Discussions often focus on activities rather than results, on the secondary rather than the substantive. Consequently many boards perform at a distressingly low percentage of their potential. Thus where opportunity for leadership is the greatest, performance turns out to be among the poorest.

"The failures of governance are not a problem of people, but of process," echo the words of John Carver, author of the must-read book *Boards That Make a Difference.*[8] Listen to his convicting lament: "Concern is often expressed through complaints over time spent on trivial items, time spent reading reams of documents, meetings that run for hours and accomplish little, committees that are window dressing for what staff wants to do, meddling in administration, staff that are more in control of board agenda than is the board, reactivity rather than proactivity, an executive committee becoming the de facto board, not knowing what is going on, rubber stamping staff recommendations, and lack of an incisive way to evaluate the executive."[9]

Until we define our performance in terms of success and failure, and what is and what is not worth doing in terms of the mission of the organization, we will continue to be dysfunctional. Our focus must not be exclusively on the present, but on the future; not on what our board is, but on what it can become. Longevity by itself is indistinguishable from vegetation.

Peter Drucker states categorically, "All nonprofit boards have one thing in common—they do not work." If this is true, why? In most cases we fail to teach people principles of group process and creativity. Here is where we can make the most extensive use of the creative techniques featured in chapters 8–14, 17: Problem-solving, brainstorming, plussing, objection-countering, gaming, mind-mapping, and storyboarding are ideal for this context.

We desperately need an upgrade in how governing boards govern. In fact, I believe it is immoral to dislodge a responsible person from his family to come and waste precious time in a nonproductive board or committee meeting.

> **"Elephants never stop growing and have been known to remain standing after they die. The same could be said of some churches."**
>
> —Fast Company

Programming

This aspect of ministry refers to special events for evangelistic outreach—for example, a "living Christmas tree," a musical at Easter, and so forth. In upstate New York a church featured a sports day every year. The day included hunting, fishing, and golfing—activities in which special awards were given in each division. The day always concluded with an evening banquet featuring the testimony of an outdoor specialist or a well-known athlete. This effort to penetrate the community was the highlight of that church's year, and many came to faith in Christ as a result.

In my own pastorate many years ago our small church grew in community stature through a Saturday evening concert series we sponsored. To that town, at that time, the idea was new and attractive. Of course, musical concerts or any other artistic presentation demand excellence in programming.

Cultural events can reach out to people who might never come into contact with a local church any other way. For example, an Arts Fest hosted by Calvary Baptist Church in New York City involves a segment of the artistic community that surrounds that church. Many Christian lectureships are featured, bringing men and women of distinction in their fields of expertise to the attention of the community with great enrichment.

Men's and women's retreats can be real winners, especially if well planned and featuring people who can speak to the needs of the group from a strong biblical perspective. These can be planned for a day or a weekend. Sometimes a hotel is appropriate, other times a camp or resort setting works best. Advance planning and creative programming are the keys to making these effective.

A word of caution about events, however: Beware of the *pseudo-event*. This term was used by the late Daniel Boorstin, long-time history professor at the University of Chicago and director of the Smithsonian Museum of History and the Library of Congress. It describes the man-made ethical or spiritual images we concoct, not because they are good, but because they are merely entertaining. Too much of our church life imitates this art form of the commercial world.

Boorstin says we suffer unwittingly from our own idolatry. The more images we present, the more unattractive we become. Why? "Our images suggest arrogance: in them we set ourselves up as a mold for the world. . . . The image . . . limited, concrete, and oversimplified—inevitably seems narrow and unadaptable."[10]

This warning reminds us that our people need a dynamism, a free-flowing sense of pulsating real life. We need to ponder the question, When people come to see our productions, will they also feed on spiritual food?

Administration

For all our inventiveness we are still primitive when it comes to designing and operating effective organizations. A perceptive businessman once reflected, "I have discovered a new reason for believing the church is a divine institution. No other organization could survive if managed so haphazardly. This is proof positive that God must be in it." Ouch! This man's perceptive (though biting) observation reflects a reality that is all too often true.

To many, this matter of organization is thought of as so much "administrivia." But to anyone seriously involved in the work of the Lord, organizational creativity either makes or breaks the ministry. James D. Berkley enunciated this principle clearly: "In the final analysis, church management comes down to service: the willingness to do what it takes to make ministry happen through others."[11]

So how would your church or organization score against this criterion? Is it doing what it takes to accomplish effective service through others? Several components of administrative excellence are worth highlighting:

The Office

The nerve center of the operation needs to be well-organized and run with efficiency. Our unspoken message in this unit should say, "We are here to serve you." But we need to be sure someone helpful is there when we say they will be. Otherwise they are not truly serving. A people-friendly ministry is a unique business with a compassionate heart.

The Telephone

Providing office hours, times of services, and the phone number for a person to call in case of an emergency is essential. Avoid answering machines whenever possible. Personal is powerful, and people in today's high-tech society need high-touch ministry.

The Receptionist

A warm, lively first impression and personal responsiveness in this function is indispensable. This individual needs to be the best-informed person on location, knowing how to connect callers or visitors with the resources they need. A strong personal orientation is essential, combined with a strong ability to answer questions being asked.

The Secretary/Administrative Assistant

In my judgment, the function of this person needs to be high priority. An effective assistant can often increase the impact of a church substantially.

The Learning/Resource Center

Books, tapes, films, videos, and other media should be available for borrowing or on-site use. A knowledgeable librarian is a valuable asset here.

Every administration labors under the spell of assumptions that are so taken for granted they are never questioned, even (or perhaps especially) by those most intimately involved. This is why every organization occasionally needs an outside perspective, a fresh pair of eyes, people who are not anesthetized by routine commitment and involvement. Sometimes it is far easier to see the faults of other churches or ministries than to see one's own deficiencies.

One of the most neglected areas of administration centers on succession. Indeed, this may become the number-one issue of church leaders in the next decade, as the "old guard" begins to turn over.

Yet it's interesting to ask pastors what their vision is for their congregations. Quite often you will hear a fairly lofty and noble mission articulated, one that, if accomplished, would certainly make a difference in the community. But more often than not, that vision statement sees no further than the end of the pastor's tenure. What are you doing that will outlive you? What is your church's vision, not just for the next five or ten years while you are there, but for the next twenty-five to fifty years, after you're long gone?

Remember Peter Drucker's advice: The best way to predict the future is to create it. Therefore we need to begin *now* to raise up a new generation of leaders who understand and embrace the church's mission. We may ignore the fact that we will falter in the mission unless we constantly employ understudies for each and every function.

Discipleship

In his classic volume, *Daily with the King,* W. Glynn Evans discusses Jesus' call to His disciples, "Follow me, and I will make you fishers of men" (Matt. 4:19). "That call has to do with the *ownership of rights,* and it is addressed only to those who have responded to the first call [Matt. 11:28, Come unto me . . . I will give you rest . . . Take my yoke . . . learn of me]. Next to the problem of sin, the problem of rights will be my most grievous. Here the battle may be fiercer and the struggle longer. Nevertheless, Jesus Christ insists that all Christians enroll as quickly as possible as His disciples."[12]

Our overuse of the discipleship concept has tended to erode the true intent of our Lord. Discipleship is not a program but a *process* that must be geared to the individual or group involved. People need basic exposure to the demands of discipleship, the cost, and the rewards.

They also need to build on that foundation. Disciple efforts are often considerable for young people and young believers. But what do we have to help a thirty-five-year-old Christian continue to grow in grace and in the knowledge of our Lord? Or individuals of any other age? Or shut-ins and those who are disabled? Consider carefully the use of printed materials, questionnaires, and one-on-one discipleship and groups.

Discipleship exists to bring people to their full maturity in Christ (Col. 1:28–29). Everyone in ministry is compelled to ask, What am I doing today that will guarantee my impact for Christ in the next generation? The New Testament is clear; there are only two things God will take off this planet: His Word and His people. A lasting legacy is ensured by building His Word into the lives of people.

A great unresolved problem in the evangelical church today is that we are not doing what the risen Head of the church commanded us to do: to make disciples (Matt. 28:19–20). A New Testament church must be more than a preaching center, it must be a discipleship center—where people come to faith, are built up in the faith, and are equipped to live and reproduce their faith.

My growing conviction is that while you cannot build a great church without great preaching, neither can you build a great church by preaching alone. One of the leading expositors of our generation admitted, "I learned how to build a great church, but I never learned how to build great people." Perhaps this is why, for many, there is so little fulfillment in ministry. The fruit does not remain.

What is discipleship? It's not a label for an empty bottle. Your concept of discipleship will determine what you do. Biblically a disciple is three things: (a) *a learner* (Matt. 11:25–30). Therefore perpetuate the learning process (Phil. 4:9) and develop lifelong learners. (b) *A follower* (Mark 2:14; 3:14). Therefore provide a model (1 Cor. 11:1). (c) *A reproducer of a lifestyle* (Matt. 28:20). Therefore be careful what you produce.

The characteristics of a disciple are also evident from Scripture. A disciple is obedient (John 8:31–32), loving (13:34–35), and fruitful (15:8, 16). In light of these biblical parameters, the discipleship question becomes clear: Am I developing learning followers who are reproducing Jesus Christ in the lives of others?

Writing

Oswald Chambers, one of the most frequently read Christian writers, wrote, "The author or speaker from whom you learn the most is not the one who teaches you something you didn't know before but the one who helps you take a truth with which you have quietly struggled, give it expression and speak it clearly and boldly."[13] This is a helpful articulation of what good writing does. Writing is the right words in the right place at the right time.

When God etched His commandments on tablets at Mount Sinai, He set the precedent for preserving His Word. When God wanted to communicate with humanity in the twenty-first century, He wrote His message in a book. The printed page never flinches. It is never tempted to compromise. It's a visitor who gets inside the home and stays there. It works long after we are dead. It is bait permanently left in the water.

In our modern world, writing is still a live option for effective communication. What we write and how we do it is determined by our creativity quotient. "Not to be fortified with good ideas is to be victimized by bad ones."[14] Regarding writing, here are some suggestions to consider:

Query the publishers to determine what they are looking for. Editors and publishers who live daily with the needs of the reading public in mind can be trusted to steer a prospective writer toward a needed topic. They know the market, the readership, and what will sell. Don't write a book and then go looking for a publisher. Talk to publishers first about your idea for a book.

Write articles, because someday they may turn into books. Many writers envision their byline on a book jacket, but nearly all published authors started out with smaller pieces, often in obscure publications.

Ask for realistic and critical evaluation of your writing. Look on this as an educational opportunity. Rejection slips are part of the learning process.

Good writing involves rewriting. Write something down, then make it better. Then rewrite it to make it the best you can. And learn to interpret what rejection means when you submit a sample of your manuscript to an editor. Rejection is not always a comment on the writing style but more a matter of timing or placement. Always, the craft of writing demands rethinking, reworking.

"Young man," H. G. Wells quipped to an aspiring writer, "you have a style before you have a story, and God help you." Writing must be organized, but the outline must not show. It must be an interesting presentation but never a gingerbread house of fancy words.

Target your writing for an audience. Creative writing always stands in the shoes of the reader. Some sermons are the worst in terms of ill-aimed material. Remember, you are an idea person before you are a wordsmith. So who is interested in your ideas? If no one is, you have no audience. If someone "ought" to be, then how can you make what you have to say interesting and engaging for *them* (not for you)?

Learn to write for the unchurched. Originality does not mean discovering something new. There's nothing new under the sun (Eccles. 1:9). Unfortunately too many of us are still preaching mostly to the choir. We need a C. S. Lewis in the twenty-first century, someone who can reconnect with the language and thinking of our generation.

Public Relations

The secular advertising industry employs some of the most creative minds in our society. Most of our know-how about the creative process comes from them. But while we can learn from them, we must be careful not to imitate them unwisely. Christian organizations are being scrutinized as never before. So consider the following:

- Spend cautiously. Better to have one good piece in print than twenty poor ones.
- Avoid the Saturday church page. Few people apart from other preachers and regular attendees read it.
- If you run an ad, try to place it in the sports or another specialty section. Use community weeklies that have local outlets.
- If you run TV ads, timing is crucial—for example, between segments or just after key athletic events. Know the personnel at the station and do your homework.
- Devise a quality piece to be given to visitors that explains the uniqueness of your church and what it provides for various constituencies such as families, singles, seniors, others. Pinpoint what your congregation has to offer that meets the special needs of visitors reading the piece.
- The optimum promotion is personal word-of-mouth, satisfied members who exude enthusiasm.

- Issue a regular information piece with fresh news that contains short testimonials, pictorials or graphic design, and crisp prose to keep people up to date on your doings. A resource newsletter for leaders is an invaluable tool.
- Press conferences and other media coverage can be a powerful means of community outreach. But you must know what is newsworthy. You must also get to know reporters, keep to their deadlines, and follow current events to maximize the benefits.

Positive promotion spills over far beyond printed ads. Youth activities have long been advanced through colorful handouts with cartoons and clever graphics that the kids themselves love to produce. A recent example I saw was a brochure to publicize Eagle Lake Camp, a thriving youth ministry of The Navigators. The campers themselves were encouraged to submit drawings depicting their favorite aspects of the camping experience. Then the best ones were chosen and compiled into an attractive brochure for general mailing. The results were great.

In public relations never forget the creative personal touch. Interviews with someone who has a pertinent story to tell are powerful. Ideally their telling of it must be short, questions should be specific, and all dialogue should be directed toward the event or ministry the story is highlighting.

For older folks a personal invitation to a given function is particularly effective. If an anniversary of a department or other part of the ministry is coming up, perhaps dedicating a specific musical number or other part of a larger meeting may underscore the event.

Networking with other Christian groups can also benefit everyone. An annual sunrise service or Christmas event, for example, can unite the community and underscore our relationship with other believers. Friendliness should be the rule here; but manipulation or lobbying to secure visibility sends the wrong message. The difference between manipulation and leadership is motive. In your attempt to be creative in public relations, don't lose your credibility.

The act of placing one's ministry into the marketplace of ideas always waves a caution flag. Jesus Christ taught us to be as shrewd as snakes but as innocent as doves (Matt. 10:16). This is the grid through which we must filter all of our public relations.

Worship

Worship is a personal response to divine revelation. God has spoken, and He has not stuttered. When the Samaritan woman sought to embroil the Savior in an argument about worshiping God, He redirected her attention from the *place* for worship to the *person* to be worshiped, with these words: "Yet a time is coming and has now come when the true worshipers will worship the Father in spirit and truth, for they are the kind of worshipers the Father seeks" (John 4:23). Thus we grieve the Holy Spirit every time we spurn what He seeks.

Jesus' words teach us that worship is an individual heart response. However, our experience often takes place in a corporate setting. Most pastors have uncovered the importance of leading their parishioners to discover the power of an encounter with the living God. Unfortunately their seminaries have often provided minimal training in the art of leading worship.

Meaningful and edifying worship is always the product of long-range planning. Choosing songs and deciding the agenda for the service a few days before it takes place suggests amateurism and is totally untrustworthy in terms of results.

Have you ever noticed that the word *worship* is a verb? It indicates a response to God, and it requires active participation of our whole being. When I was a pastor in Fort Worth, Texas, an elder told me he was incapable of singing, yet I noticed his lips moving whenever we sang the hymns. So I asked him about it. His response was significant: "Pastor, I haven't worshiped unless I have personally responded to my Lord."

Our minds and emotions need to be drawn away from the oppressive and insistent gravity of our world and lifted toward the light and life of Christ. When worship becomes predictable, it is simply a time-filler, uninteresting and devoid of impact. By using creatively thought-provoking and challenging presentations, worship can arouse and enliven one's relationship with the Lord. Never, never should it become entertainment or a spectator sport.

Themes should be chosen so that every part of a church service contributes to the overall objective: to worship God in the beauty of holiness.

This model presupposes that the preaching and the musical leadership are prepared in advance. Good worship embraces a variety of means to adore the Lord. Music, prayer, testimony, silence, meditation, sermon—each should invite participation. Howard Stevenson reminds us, "In responding to God we should be open to using every expression of beauty and genius which are reflections of his own nature."[15]

The entire service should suffuse the congregation with the realization that God is the audience and we are the participants. This avoids turning the service into a recreational event in which we put up number signs to indicate our evaluation of the performances. Worship that impacts people must also be geared to the educational and cultural tastes of the audience. Whenever possible, educate your people upward—musically, theologically, and esthetically. Never dumb down your audience.

Leadership Development

A profound yet unresolved problem confronting the church today is an "unemployment" problem. There are too many drones in the divine hive. We need to be very careful that we do not charge God foolishly. He is still in the process of dispensing gifts, but we are not in the process of developing gifts.

The searching test of any organization is its ability to generate and develop its own leadership. God never calls a ministry into existence without providing all the resources with which to fulfill the mission. Therefore the task confronting us is twofold: to determine what we want to develop and to develop what we have determined.

Let's suppose we have determined to develop people with these characteristics:

- *Committed* unreservedly to Jesus Christ, to the body of Christ, and to the work of Christ.
- *Competent* individuals who know truth thoroughly, who feel truth deeply, and who live truth consistently.
- *Communicative* people, able to read, write, think, and speak the truth clearly.
- *Creative* individuals, who are flexible, resourceful, and intentional.

Are we finding these people? Not usually, because we do not expect to. Then are we developing them? If so, how? How do we develop what we have determined? Let me suggest a couple of ways.

First, by enlistment. How you enlist a person will largely determine how he will serve. Negatively, eliminate all public pleas for volunteers, all last-minute appointments, and every form of personal arm-twisting. Positively, assess people's giftedness, the contribution God has designed them, indeed called them, to make. Then establish a placement committee whose primary task is to match individuals with functions based on giftedness.

Second, by training. All training must be realistic, continual, and personal. The goal: no job without training. Never ask people to do you a favor, but to join a fellowship. Inform them of the demands of the job and what they can expect by way of training. Your motto should be, "We expect much of you, and you may expect much of us." Then ask them to pray about it. "Don't tell us yes until you've told God yes, and don't tell us no until you've told Him no."

Once you have determined what you want to develop, keep in mind these two constants of enlistment and training. Development goals *always* dictate how you enlist and train.

Leadership training must embrace two areas: content and methodology. The inventory of a creative Christian leader should include basic Bible knowledge and a personal grasp of the doctrinal commitments of the ministry. Preparation for the skills of the task at hand must also be shared.

Every individual is potentially a creative person. When he or she is free to express this intrinsic energy, everyone gains. The best training is on the job. It ought to include junior boards, or some means of raising up a new generation of leaders who have both experience and commitment to the vision of the mission.

Some basic leadership development principles: (a) Develop leaders in line with their spiritual and natural gifts. (b) Motivate people to employ their abilities through assessment, mentoring, and coaching. (c) Structure leadership training as a privilege, not a duty. (d) Help individuals feel comfortable in whatever aspect of ministry they have. (e) Ensure that the supervisors understand how to manage people as well as how *not* to manage them. (f) Hide the organization and highlight the Lord whom we all serve.

Vision

Two California leaders of leaders, Warren Bennis and Burt Nanus, climaxed their bestselling volume, *Leaders,* with these words: "The absence or ineffectiveness of leadership implies the absence of vision, a dreamless society, and this will result, at best, in the maintenance of the status quo, or, at worst, in the disintegration of our society because of lack of purpose and cohesion."[16] If this is true for the secular world, how much more so for a fellowship of believers who walk by faith?

Creative ministries move ahead on tracks that have been laid to the horizon. Someone must scout the wilderness ahead and erect the signposts; otherwise there is real danger of defaulting and decomposing. Our challenge in Christian ministry is to determine how to read the unexplored territory, how to validate a leader's convictions, how to distinguish a God-given creative thought from a castle in the air.

A vision is a mental picture of a desired future state, the ultimate goal. It is what you want to achieve, a definition of your purpose. It is the heart of leadership, which earns respect, and that in turn produces trust. Vision also energizes character, mobilizes it, gives it direction and focus, and makes it productive. Without vision, character sits idle, like a piece of workmanship that is admired but not used.

Individuals embrace two kinds of vision—personal and institutional. If these are not congruent and compatible, they will be competitive and conflicted. In that case both individuals and institutions lose out, because the individual will not be fulfilled and the institution will not be served.

Ministries prosper when their participants are drawn to a common belief that this particular group is the best to fill a special need or reach a given audience. Thus casting a vision and convincing the constituents are the essence of true leadership.

A number of factors are inherent in a genuinely inspiring vision. First, it must have some "stretch" in terms of challenge and cost. Vision always starts with where we are now and dares us to reach out beyond where we expected to go. But we have to be convinced that it is doable.

Second, the vision must be kept before the people to elicit their ownership. Each one of us instinctively asks, What good will this vision do for me and my interests? We have to like what we see. It must be trustworthy, plausible, and worthy of our investment.

Third, the vision must keep up with the times and the needs of the community. Obviously it must meet basic criteria for obedience to the Great Commission, but in accomplishing that objective it must fit this community, at this time. Therefore regular evaluation and revision are inevitably needed.

George Bernard Shaw liked to say, "I am a dreamer. Some men see things as they are and ask why; I dream of things that never were and ask, why not?"

Church history teaches us that the visions God has given to His chosen leaders have always been transmitted to the next generation, like a torch passed from one runner to the next in a relay race. Visions are all-consuming, deep-rooted compulsions, and the Scriptures teach us that they are passed on through mentoring. Moses had his Joshua; Naomi had Ruth; Elizabeth contributed to Mary; Barnabas affirmed Paul; and Paul developed Timothy. So who is your Timothy, your Mary?

One of the best models for mentoring is an Old Testament classic, Elijah and Elisha. Many Bible students think of the fearless Elijah as a loner, but his protégé Elisha had been learning and absorbing the heartbeat of the prophet. When Elijah asked Elisha, "Tell me, what can I do for you before I am taken from you?" Elisha's request was, "Let me inherit a double portion of your spirit" (2 Kings 2:9–10).

That spirit provided the widow's oil, healed Naaman the leper, made an axhead float, and completed Elijah's mission by founding a school of the prophets (2 Kings 4–6). Quite a legacy!

So the question again is, Whom are you cultivating as part of your legacy? Visions die without implantation in the life of another. There can be no success without successors.

Exercises

1. Use the following inventory to assess your church in each of the ten areas covered in this chapter:

	Poor									Outstanding
Communication	1	2	3	4	5	6	7	8	9	10
Governance	1	2	3	4	5	6	7	8	9	10
Programming	1	2	3	4	5	6	7	8	9	10
Administration	1	2	3	4	5	6	7	8	9	10
Discipleship	1	2	3	4	5	6	7	8	9	10
Writing	1	2	3	4	5	6	7	8	9	10
Public relations	1	2	3	4	5	6	7	8	9	10
Worship	1	2	3	4	5	6	7	8	9	10
Leadership development	1	2	3	4	5	6	7	8	9	10
Vision	1	2	3	4	5	6	7	8	9	10

What specifically can you do to improve in each area? Use the techniques of creativity covered in this book! And be sure to involve other leaders in both the evaluation and envisioning phases.

2. Revisit exercise number 7 at the end of chapter 4, "Kinds of Creative Thinking." How does the outcome of the inventory above affect that exercise, and vice versa?

Helpful Resources

- Barna, George. *Church Marketing: Breaking Ground for the Harvest.* Ventura, Calif.: Regal Books, 1992.
- Biehl, Bobb, and Ted W. Engstrom. *Boardroom Confidence.* Sisters, Oreg.: Questar, 1988.
- Carver, John. *Boards That Make a Difference.* San Francisco: Jossey-Bass, 1990.
- Gangel, Kenneth O., and Howard G. Hendricks. *The Christian Educator's Handbook on Teaching.* Grand Rapids: Baker Books, 1988.

- Hayford, Jack, John Killinger, and Howard Stevenson. *Mastering Worship.* Portland, Oreg.: Multnomah, 1990.
- Hendricks, Howard G. *Teaching to Change Lives.* Portland, Oreg.: Multnomah, 1987.
- Hughes, Kent, and Barbara Hughes. *Liberating Ministry from the Success Syndrome.* Wheaton, Ill.: Tyndale House Publishers, 1988.
- Morgenthaler, Sally. *Worship Evangelism.* Grand Rapids: Zondervan, 1995.
- Wiersbe, Warren W. *Preaching and Teaching with Imagination: The Quest for Biblical Ministry.* Grand Rapids: Baker Books, 1994.
- Wilkinson, Bruce H. *Teaching with Style* video series. 1994. Atlanta: Walk Thru the Bible, 1994.
- Zuck, Roy B. *Teaching as Jesus Taught.* Grand Rapids: Baker Books, 1996.
- ———. *Teaching as Paul Taught.* Grand Rapids: Baker Books, 1998.

Creativity and Leadership

The best way to predict the future is to create it.

—**PETER DRUCKER**

21

The most compelling question confronting every evangelical church today is, How do we prevent institutional dry rot? "Most human organizations that fall short of their goals do so," John W. Gardner wrote, "not because of stupidity or faulty beliefs, but because of internal decay and rigidification. They grow stiff in the joints. They get in a rut. They go to seed."[1]

Like people and plants, organizations have a life cycle. But they differ in two crucial respects: They are not predictable, and they are capable of change. The decaying process can be reversed. The cycle can occur in ten or a hundred years. Keep in mind the progression:

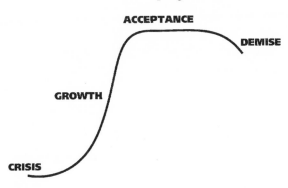

Crisis. All organizations are founded in response to a strongly perceived need. Just think of the founding of any given church, mission, seminary, or parachurch ministry such as Young Life, The Navigators, Campus Crusade for Christ, and hundreds of others. In every case, there is a period of sacrifice, servanthood, and strong community.

Growth. The dynamic of a growing organization is evident. There is always involvement, excitement, and commitment. In fact, it often grows so fast that it is compelled to become organized. This expansion is a double-edged sword. If an organization grows out of need and is modulated by that need, it is healthy, life-giving, and essential. If not, then it becomes an end rather than a means to an end, and the result is often tragedy. Structure is a necessity, as illustrated in the early church's choosing of seven leaders to handle a food-distribution problem (Acts 6:1–6).

Acceptance. Now the organization has a reputation, and that is frequently lethal. Living in the past becomes a way of life. Like Sardis (Rev. 3:1–6), the group has a name but is dead, or nearly so. Jesus warned us, "Beware when all men speak well of you" (Luke 6:26). Success often breeds an attitude of smugness, and the "lunatic fringe" increases.

Demise. Response to present need is missing. The institution remains, but the purpose blurs. Insensitivity prevails. The framework may still be there, but the mission dies. As Gardner predicted, "They grow stiff in the joints. They get in a rut. They go to seed." Like Samson, the organization may attempt to go out and do battle as before, but the leaders are unaware that the Lord has departed from them (Judg. 16:20). Now Ichabod ("the glory has departed," 1 Sam. 4:21) is the appropriate title to be written over the remains.

Once dynamic organizations have within them the seeds of decay, the people committed to them are oftentimes the last to know it. The tragedy is that many times they can detect the product in other organizations but cannot discern the process developing in their own. Formerly vibrant and impactful tools become dull, rusty, and useless. They become shadows of their former selves. Hardening of the attitudes is more devastating than hardening of the arteries.

Symptoms

Deterioration in any institution (or individual) produces warning signs. A system that is not innovating is a system that is dying. The coroner's report: death by decay. Terminal illness of an organization has at least these six symptoms.

The institution is more concerned about programs than people. People become expendable. Programs are perpetuated that no longer meet needs. W. A. Criswell, long-time pastor of the First Baptist Church of Dallas, Texas, told one of my seminary classes, "Die for a principle, not a method." Therefore the ultimate question to ask of any program is whether it is developing or destroying people. Is it a good method for another generation, with no impact on this one? We learn from the past, but we do not live in it.

Policies are many,

Principles are few,

Policies will change,

Principles never do.

The past becomes more important than the future. These organizations spend an inordinate amount of time celebrating anniversaries. They talk more about what Christ used to do here, rather than what He is doing here now, and what we are trusting Him to do here (and beyond) in the future.

"On the plains of hesitation bleach the bones of countless millions who, on the threshold of victory, sat down to wait, and in waiting, died."

—William Mounton Marston

There is more concern about preservation than propagation. Maintenance takes precedent over growth. These groups are often evangelical, but not evangelistic. They become Bible teaching centers with little or no impact on the community. They try to preserve what they have and proceed to lose it.

I evaluated a church some years ago that could not point to one adult who had made a profession of faith in Jesus Christ during the last seven years! The more you give away, the more you keep; the more you try to preserve, the more you paralyze.

There is more concern about reputation than responsibility. Demise lies just ahead of those who are more concerned about what people think than what Christ commanded. Observe where Jesus spent His time (e.g., Mark 2:13–17). *What* Christ was determined *where* He was. Most of His time was spent among the sick, not the self-righteous. He spent His energies with the people most of whom we try to avoid.

There is a greater concern for form than for function. Form must always follow function. You can overhaul the form, but if the function is not clear, the change of form will bring no significant improvement.

One must determine the difference between what is biblical and what is cultural. Having a worship team up front and placing the hymns or praise songs on a screen will change the form of worship but not necessarily the function. We easily become prisoners of our own perspectives.

There is commitment to conformity rather than change. The one is external, the other internal. Real change must emanate from within. One can make all the right formations, jump all the expected hoops, and yet remain totally unchanged. When the Holy Spirit brings internal change, the fruit remains.

And conformity can be just as deadly in regard to the present as to the past. Many of our churches today are more conformed to the pattern of our society than the precedent of the Scriptures. In truth, the world is making a greater impact on us than we are on the world.

Either way—as traditionalists or "trend-followers"—we become frozen in a slice of time. This status quo contrasts sharply with David's life described in Acts 13:36: "For when David had *served God's purpose in his own generation,* he fell asleep" (italics added). All the way to the end, he was God's man, pursuing God's agenda.

These symptoms reflect the more serious disease of spiritual dry rot. Humans develop a movement; the movement becomes a machine; the machine degenerates into a monument. In a word, the innovators can end up becoming embalmers.

"The problem is never how to get new, innovative thoughts into your mind, but how to get old ones out. Every mind is a room packed with archaic furniture. You must get the old furniture of what you know, think, and believe out before anything new can get in. Make an empty space in any corner of your mind, and creativity will instantly fill it."

—Dee Hock

Solutions

While the solutions to every organization will be unique, depending on the specific circumstances, the answers will grow out of some fundamental elements. Here are six.

Determine Your Core Values

These are the things that *must* be in order that other things *might* be. A reflective evaluation of the original mission statement is in order. A realistic probe into what has actually happened since inception, and a careful and concise gathering of what is crucial, must take place.

Devise a Set of Clear-Cut Objectives and Priorities

Your objectives determine your outcomes. You achieve that for which you aim. If you lose sight of your objectives, you concentrate on motion, but it is motion without meaning. All objectives ought to be the product of your biblical philosophy of ministry, including attention to Matthew 28:16–20; Acts 2:41–47; Ephesians 4:11–13; and 2 Timothy 2:2.

John Bright, professor of Old Testament at Union Theological Seminary in Richmond, Virginia, was lecturing in Fort Worth. At the conclusion of one of his lectures he was asked a penetrating question: "Dr. Bright, what is the primary purpose of the seminary in today's culture?" One could discern that he had been waiting for years to be asked that question, because he responded immediately. "The primary purpose of the seminary today is to unfit men and women for the ministry as commonly perceived by the churches today." What a prophetic word!

The problem is, we are all too often devoid of clear-cut objectives. What is the purpose of the church? What is the purpose of your local church? What is it that Jesus Christ is building? How have we become derailed and focused on secondary targets? These questions—and many like them—need to be asked and re-asked in our generation if the church will continue that for which the Lord designed and placed it here, namely, cutting-edge ministry.

Engage in Continual and Strategic Long-Range Planning

One's strategy is determined by asking and answering three seminal questions: Where are we? Where do we need to be? How can we get from here to there? Three things prove determinative in answering these questions: a mission statement, a philosophy of ministry, a strategic ministry plan.

Many years ago a thoughtful layman made an inflammatory statement in my presence. "Hendricks," he said, "I'm convinced the average evangelical church is doomed to mediocrity." I flinched but hesitatingly probed, "What is your evidence for that?" Like a laser beam, he shot back, "The average evangelical church does not plan to be in business very long."

I have been meditating on that pronouncement ever since. It has been doing a slow burn in my brain. I am convinced he is correct.

I asked a pastor, "What are you planning to do in the next ten years?" His response? "I don't know what I'm planning to do next Sunday, let alone the next decade." That sums up our problem.

I had the privilege of working with a group of laymen involved in a new church plant. After I introduced them to the subject of strategic planning, they sat down after much prayer and came up with a list of eight objectives for the next twelve months. Ten months later I received an enthusiastic phone call from them. "We are only ten months into our plan and six of our eight objectives are already accomplished. The other two will be completed next month. We are already updating our plan."

Unusual? Not at all. I believe where prayer and planning focus, power follows. We may not take our faith very seriously, but God does—and He is not playing church!

To be sure, all our plans need to be tentative and flexible. Let God be God. Let Him surprise and redirect you. Just make sure your plans are big enough that God can get into them. Don't limit God by your restraints. We don't plan to fail, but we often fail to plan.

Create an Effective Means of Community Penetration

The key is not being locked into one method, particularly one that was effective in a former generation, or a different socioeconomic group. It may be totally ineffective in today's setting. And this is the decision-making place where creativity makes an impact. "Lord, what do you want us to do to reach these people for Jesus?"

For example, one of the fruitful ministries I have seen is a bus pickup for certain neighborhoods. But is that necessarily appropriate for every community? We tend to universalize success. We want to make the Lord's leading for us the standard for everyone: If God led us to bus people to our church, then He is probably leading everyone to do the same. Not necessarily. In fact, it might be grossly ineffective and counterproductive in another community.

My wife, Jeanne, and I belong to a church in Dallas founded more than forty years ago to reach the business and professional leaders of our city. The membership is highly educated and generally affluent. Can you imagine a more incongruous method of ministry than to drive the church bus along the streets of North Dallas, a very affluent community where it's typical for a driveway to have a Cadillac, a BMW, or a Ferrari, and probably a fancy SUV parked? It is not the place to beep the little bus horn!

In contrast, home Bible studies make an entirely different impact in that part of the city. On occasion, people come to these classes just to see the home!

Methods of ministry must be relevant to the lifestyle. We need to embrace the motto "Nothing to prove, nothing to lose." The copycat mode must give way to truly creative thinking in order to determine what are the best means of confronting our community with the claims of Christ.

The answers are not all in. There is plenty of room for more expressions of evangelistic concern and creative methodology.

That means that if we spend too much time finding out what others are doing, rather than concentrating more closely on creative thinking for our own ministry, we can easily derail. We need a commitment to aggressive and innovative evangelism.

Accent Perpetual Recruitment and Training of Laypeople

Very few Christian organizations can afford to hang a sign on their door, "No Help Wanted." Wherever I go, the screaming need is for leadership. But in many cases there is no realistic recruitment and training program (see chapter 20, "Creativity and the Ministry").

Assessment is essential in the recruitment process. Surveys are one way of facilitating this. But there must be follow-up to the responses.

One Sunday morning I sat in church beside a gentleman who glanced at his survey and put it aside. I commented, "This isn't for you, huh?" His forthright answer disturbed me, "Oh, I filled out one of these before and nothing happened, so why should I do it again?"

The untapped source of human vitality, the unmined lode of talent, is in people like my friend who was already surveyed and thereafter neglected. Leadership is rotting in our pews.

How you recruit a person will determine how he or she serves. If your needs are great now and you are growing, they will be much greater in five to ten years. So don't ask people to take a *job*; give them an *opportunity*. Introduce them to a challenge in line with their giftedness, a ministry worthy of their investment.

Here are some worthwhile goals:

- No church member without a ministry (either inside or outside the church—or both).
- No ministry without training. Every service opportunity within a ministry should have a written description of the job and an ongoing training plan that is inviting and satisfying.
- No ministry without evaluated experience. Each member needs a chance to perform teaching or serving in whatever capacity under

the watchful eye of a supervisor. The test of a quality church is not how many members it has but what kind of involvement exists in the most exciting work God is doing on the planet. The best time to recruit is when a person becomes a member of the local church. Don't be the "Church of the Sacred Rest." What is the purpose of becoming a member if one is not actively involved?

For every job we need adequate training. First-rate organizations always spend a substantial percentage of their budget on training. First Corinthians 12:4–7 makes it transparent that God gave to every believer a spiritual gift, not so they could spectate in the stands, but to participate on the playing field. Paul also informed us that God gives gifts to men and women, and gifted men and women to the church. Why? To equip the saints for *their* work of ministry (Eph. 4:11–12). That involves training ten people to do the work, not doing the work of ten people. It is a ministry of multiplication, not addition.

The missing ingredient of the contemporary church is the training of laypeople for leadership. Two aspects must be recognized: church work and the work of the church. Church work (e.g., teaching, ushering, janitoring, and so forth) can be handled most effectively by a small coterie of people. The work of the church—that is, what members do at home, in the community, and in the marketplace—demands that *every* Christian be involved.

Unfortunately we are not equipping laypeople to be laypeople in their respective spheres of ministry. Most of them do not even know they are in the ministry. Many perceive their daily job as their penalty, not a possibility for Christ's service. They figure they have to do a forty- or fifty-hour workweek as the price to get to the church, where they can have "a real ministry." Nonprofessionals are not being equipped for ministry, either within or without the local churches.

The test of virility in an organization, I repeat, is its ability to generate and groom its own leadership. The best leaders come from within an organization. The church does not need to go outside itself to discover leaders who can function within its sphere. God does not call a church into existence and then abandon it to inadequate human direction. He dispenses His gifts; but lamentably, we often fail to develop them.

Cultivate the Ability of Our People to Trust God

In the Gospels the only thing our Lord ever rebuked His disciples for was their lack of faith (Mark 4:40). He never scored them for not having their tunics tucked in or their sandals shined, or for their hair being too long. However, "without faith, it is impossible to please God," the writer of Hebrews assured us (Heb. 1:6). Jesus remarked, "Without me you can do nothing" (John 15:6). The awful finality of those words! Something? No! *Nothing!* Everything must come from God; nothing originates with us.

God specializes in doing the impossible. So we are compelled to ask, What are you trusting God for today that only God can do? When He does it, you will never be able to say you accomplished it; only, "To *God* be the glory; great things *He* has done!"

Such a mandate often provokes an alibi: "But it's not my responsibility." Wrong! The body of Christ works best as a unit in which all the parts are involved in making the body work at its optimum level (1 Cor. 12). We dare not compromise or dilute our divinely given job assignments.

Churches are subject to the deadening forces that afflict all human institutions: an attachment to time-honored ways, preoccupation with vested interests, and an excessively narrow definition of what is relevant and important.

These cataracts develop a functional blindness to our own defects. We are not impotent because we cannot solve our problems, but because we refuse to see them. Traditionalists, unfortunately, often believe that foolishness frozen into custom is preferable to foolishness fresh off the vine!

Exercises

1. Where is your church in the organizational life cycle shown at the beginning of this chapter?

2. Who are the leaders in your congregation? Use mind-mapping (see chapter 14) or create a storyboard (see chapter 17) to identify who they are. Next to each person's name, identify the top three strengths or abilities that person has to contribute to the church.

3. Is there anyone in your church who you believe has leadership ability but is not exercising it? Why not? Use the strategy of objection-countering (see chapter 12) to find an answer to this question. What is preventing leaders from contributing to your church effectively?

4. Use brainstorming (see chapter 9) to generate ideas for the development, training, and placing of your leaders. Here are a few "teasers" to get you started:
   - Books
   - Motion pictures
   - Learning adventures
   - Visiting experts
   - Critical incident debriefings
   - Focus groups

Helpful Resources

- Finzel, Hans. *The Top Ten Mistakes Leaders Make.* Wheaton, Ill.: Victor Books, 1994.
- ———. *Empowered Leaders.* Nashville: Word, 1998.
- Firestien, Roger. *Leading on the Creative Edge.* Colorado Springs: Piñon Press, 1996.

Be Creative!

Are you in earnest? Seize this very minute. What you can do or think you can, begin it.

—Johann W. Von Goethe

22

How do we Christians inform our generation about the most important life-saver, the critical linchpin, of their eternal lives? Os Guinness does a masterful job of addressing this concern.

> Modern cities make people closer yet stranger at once; modern weapons bring their users to the point of impotence and destruction simultaneously; modern media promise facts but deliver fantasies; modern education introduces mass schooling but fosters sub-literacy; modern technologies of communication encourage people to speak more and say less and to hear more and listen less; modern lifestyles offer do-it-yourself freedom but slavishly follow fads; modern styles of relationships make people hungry for intimacy and authenticity but more fearful than ever of phoniness, manipulation and power games.... How do we speak to an age made spiritually deaf by its skepticism and morally color-blind by its relativism?[1]

Never in all the centuries of human history has the gospel of Jesus Christ been confronted with the massive firepower of spiritual counterattacks as has our own generation. More believers in Jesus Christ have been tortured and put to death around the world during this so-called "civilized" twentieth century than in all previous centuries combined. Meanwhile, during the past two and a half decades, once-Christian America has overseen the destruction of some forty million unborn babies. And every secular voice seems to reinforce the blasphemy that humans—not God—are the rulers of all; and that God—if He is there—cares nothing about human beings.

For us whose spirits have been reborn by His grace, the challenge intensifies. Divine energy flows from the Holy Spirit like heavy-duty power lines from one hydroelectric plant to the next. But power lines in themselves are not beautiful. Only the end product, such as a lamp, which uses that power, can make the power visible, attractive, and beneficial.

Most of us have readily abandoned outmoded methods of witness. "Sandwich boards" striding the streets with warnings of doom or airplanes writing the gospel in the sky can never reach our modern secluded population. Behind their dark sunglasses and booming earphones, they pedal down bike routes and speed along interstates sealed in their own spiritually confused world. To reach our disoriented generation we *must* think and act creatively.

The nonconformist who simply wishes to show he is different, and the counter-conformist who opposes what others do—right or wrong—are like three-dollar-bills to our savvy society, which, though it is lost, hungers for authenticity. A willingness to be genuine is the tap root from which true creativity sprouts.

Let the well-worn words of St. Francis of Assisi's old prayer sink slowly into your thinking: "Lord, give me the *courage* to change those things that should be changed, the *strength* to accept the things that cannot be changed, and the *wisdom* to know the difference."

Courage, strength, wisdom. All these resources our God has promised. They come from Him. They work through His power. And they accomplish His purposes. May we claim them and use them with creative brilliance to breach the walls of ignorance and weakness in our world.

Exercises

1. What's the most important idea, thought, or skill that you gained by reading this book?
2. Look back to the list of benefits of creativity in the introductory chapter. How have you benefitted as a result of focusing on the topic and practice of creativity?
3. What action are you prepared to take—as an individual and/or as an organization—as a result of reading this book?

Endnotes

Preface

1. John W. Gardner, *No Easy Victories* (New York: Harper & Row, 1968), 49.
2. Thomas Edison, quoted in "Potpourri," *Marriage Partnership* 4 (May–June 1987).
3. Daniel Golemon, Paul Kaufinon, and Michael Ray, *The Creative Spirit* (New York: Dutton, 1992), 58.
4. Norman Cousins, *Human Options* (New York: Norton, 1981), 100.

Chapter 1: Creativity—Who Needs It?

1. G. K. Chesterton, *The Everlasting Man* (New York: Dodd, Mead, 1925), 319–20.
2. Tony Buzan, *Use Both Sides of Your Brain*, 3d ed. (New York: Dutton, 1991), 28.
3. Bob Buford, *Game Plan* (Grand Rapids: Zondervan, 1997), 42.
4. Graham Wallas, quoted in Marlene D. LeFever, "Help for the Hopelessly Uncreative," *Discipleship Journal* 48 (1988): 27–28.
5. Stanley Marcus, "Enemy of Creative Thinking," *Dallas Morning News*, 6 October 1987, 11A.

6. Dorothy Sayers, *Creed or Chaos?* (New York: Harcourt, Brace, 1949), 5–6 (italics hers).

Chapter 2: Creativity—What Is It?

1. C. S. Lewis, *The Quotable Lewis*, ed. Wayne Martindale and Jerry Root (Wheaton, Ill.: Tyndale, 1989), 135 (italics his).
2. George Marsden, "The Way We Were and Are," *Books & Culture* (November–December 1997): 19.
3. Eugene Peterson, *Earth and Altar* (Downers Grove, Ill.: InterVarsity, 1985), 18.
4. Roger Firestien, *Leading on the Creative Edge* (Colorado Springs: Piñon, 1996), 15.

Chapter 3: Creativity—Is It Biblical?

1. A. W. Tozer, *The Knowledge of the Holy* (1962; reprint, Lincoln, Nebr.: Back to the Bible Broadcast, 1971), 9.
2. Carl F. H. Henry, *A Plea for Evangelical Demonstration* (Grand Rapids: Baker, 1971), 14.
3. John Calvin, quoted in Frank Gaebelein, *The Christian, the Arts, and the Truth*, ed. D. Bruce Lockerbie (Portland, Oreg.: Multnomah, 1985), 76.
4. J. B. Phillips, *Your God Is Too Small* (New York: Macmillan, 1961).
5. Leland Ryken, *Culture and Christian Perspective* (Portland, Oreg.: Multnomah, 1986), 14.
6. Cousins, *Human Options*, 71.
7. Ryken, *Culture and Christian Perspective*, 65–66.
8. Peterson, *Earth and Altar*, 128.
9. C. S. Lewis, *The World's Last Night* (New York: Harcourt, Brace, Jovanovich, 1960), 9.
10. Paul Brand and Philip Yancey, *Fearfully and Wonderfully Made* (Grand Rapids: Zondervan, 1980), 10.
11. Dorothy Sayers, *The Mind of the Maker* (New York: Harper & Row, 1968), 34.

12. Gaebelein, *The Christian, the Arts, and the Truth*, 17.

13. Raymond Ortlund, *A Passion for God* (Wheaton, Ill.: Crossway, 1994), 207.

14. Eugene Peterson, *Traveling Light* (Colorado Springs: Helmers & Howard, 1988), 170.

15. Buford, *Game Plan*, 67–68.

16. Cheryl Forbes, *Imagination: Embracing a Theology of Wonder* (Portland, Oreg.: Multnomah, 1986), 17, 19 .

17. Eugene Peterson, *The Message* (Colorado Springs: NavPress, 1993), 473.

Chapter 4: Kinds of Creative Thinking

1. Betty Edwards, *Drawing on the Right Side of the Brain*, rev. ed. (New York: Putnam's Sons, 1989), 40.

2. Ibid., 46.

3. Maria Montessori, *The Absorbent Mind*, trans. Claude A. Claremont (New York: Dell, 1979).

4. James C. Collins and Jerry I. Porras, *Built to Last* (New York: HarperCollins, 1994).

Chapter 5: Characteristics of Creative People

1. Silvano Arieti, *The Magic Synthesis* (New York: Basic, 1976), chapter 14.

2. See Howard Gardner, *Frames of Mind: The Theory of Multiple Intelligences* (New York: Basic, 1983).

3. Peterson, *Earth and Altar*, 83.

4. For additional material on mentoring see Howard G. Hendricks, *As Iron Sharpens Iron* (Chicago: Moody, 1996).

Chapter 7: The Practice of Creativity

1. Aaron Copland, *What to Listen for in Music* (New York: McGraw-Hill, 1989), 33–100.

2. Paul Harvey, *Frontier Magazine* (August, 1981).
3. Roy B. Zuck, *Teaching as Paul Taught* (Grand Rapids: Baker, 1998), 182.

Chapter 8: Creative Problem-Solving

1. *His*, February 1984, inside back cover.
2. "Up from the Depths," *Dallas Morning News*, 12 January 1998, 1C.
3. Warren Bennis and Patricia Ward Birderman, *Organizing Genius: The Secrets of Creative Collaboration* (Reading, Mass.: Addison-Wesley), 196–97.
4. Peterson, *Earth and Altar,* 80.
5. Pierce J. Howard, *The Owner's Manual for the Brain* (Austin, Tex.: Leornian, 1994), 292.

Chapter 9: Brainstorming

1. Alex F. Osborne, *Applied Imagination,* 3d. ed. (New York: Scribner's Sons, 1961).
2. Edward de Bono, *Lateral Thinking* (New York: HarperCollins, 1990).

Chapter 11: Five-Sensing

1. For further details see Ricard M. Destack, *The Brain* (New York: Bantam, 1984).
2. H. R. Rookmaker, *Modem Art and the Death of a Culture* (Downers Grove, Ill.: InterVarsity, 1970), 202.

Chapter 14: Mind-Mapping

1. Howard, *The Owner's Manual for the Brain,* 294.

Chapter 15: Roles

1. Roger von Oech, *A Kick in the Seat of the Pants* (New York: Harper & Row, 1986).

Chapter 16: Thinking Hats

1. Edward de Bono, *Six Thinking Hats: The Power of Focused Thinking* (New York: Little, Brown, 1986).

Chapter 18: Barriers to Creativity

1. Neil Postman, *Amusing Ourselves to Death* (New York: Viking-Penguin, 1985), 155.
2. Cousins, *Human Options,* 31.
3. Gardner, *No Easy Victories,* 153–62.
4. Ibid., 55.
5. John W. Gardner, *Excellence* (New York: Harper, 1961).

Chapter 19: Creativity and Your Family

1. Glenn Stanton, *Why Marriage Matters* (Colorado Springs: Piñon, 1997), 17–18.
2. Selma Fraiberg, *The Magic Years* (New York: Scribner's, 1959), 54–55.
3. Ibid., 55.
4. Gardner, *No Easy Victories,* 71.
5. Ron Blue and Judy Blue, *Raising Money-Smart Kids* (Nashville: Nelson, 1992).
6. Ted Ward, *Values Begin at Home* (Wheaton, Ill.: Victor, 1979), 21.
7. Ibid., 48.
8. Eric Buehrer, *Charting Your Family's Course* (Wheaton, Ill.: Victor, 1994), 73.
9. Ibid., 77.

Chapter 20: Creativity and the Ministry

1. Martin Thornton, *Spiritual Direction* (Boston: Cowley, 1984), 27.
2. Eugene Peterson, *The Contemplative Pastor* (Waco, Tex.: Word, 1989), 441.
3. Helmut Thielicke, source unknown.

4. John R. W. Stott, interview by the author, Houston, Texas.

5. Henry Beer, quoted in Neal Templin, "Mall Designer Is Master of (ersatz) Regional Flavor," *Wall Street Journal*, 31 December 1997, B1.

6. Carl F. H. Henry, *Carl Henry at His Best* (Portland, Oreg.: Multnomah, 1989), 152.

7. Philip Yancey, *The Jesus I Never Knew* (New York: HarperCollins, 1995), 234.

8. John Carver, *Boards That Make a Difference* (San Francisco: Jossey-Bass, 1990).

9. Ibid., xiii.

10. Daniel Boorstin, *The Image* (New York: Atheneum, 1975), 244.

11. James D. Berkley, *Managing Church Management* (Portland, Oreg.: Multnomah, 1990), 165.

12. W. Glynn Evans, *Daily with the King* (Chicago: Moody, 1979), 170–71 (italics his).

13. Oswald Chambers, *My Utmost for His Highest* (Toronto: McClelland and Stewart, 1935), reading for December 15.

14. Carl F. H. Henry, *Twilight of a Great Civilization* (Wheaton, Ill.: Crossway, 1988), 11.

15. Howard Stevenson, *Mastering Worship* (Portland, Oreg.: Multnomah, 1990), 103.

16. Warren Bennis and Burt Nanus, *Leaders: The Strategies for Taking Charge* (New York: Harper & Row, 1985), 228.

Chapter 21: Creativity and Leadership

1. Gardner, *No Easy Victories*, 39.

Chapter 22: Be Creative!

1. Os Guinness, *The Gravedigger File* (Downers Grove, Ill.: InterVarsity, 1983).

Bibliography

Bennis, Warren, and Burt Nanus. *Leaders: The Strategies for Taking Charge.* New York: Harper & Row, 1985.

Bennis, Warren, and Patricia Ward Birderman. *Organizing Genius: The Secrets of Creative Collaboration.* Reading, Mass: Addison-Wesley Publishing Co., 1997.

Brand, Paul, and Philip Yancey. *Fearfully and Wonderfully Made.* Grand Rapids: Zondervan Publishing House, 1980.

Buzan, Tony. *Make the Most of Your Mind.* New York: Simon & Schuster, 1984.

———. *Use Both Sides of Your Brain.*3d ed. New York: E. P. Dutton & Co., 1991.

Csikszentmihalyi, Mihaly. *Flow: The Psychology of Optimal Experience.* New York: HarperCollins, 1990.

Collins, James C., and Jerry I. Porras. *Built to Last.* New York: HarperCollins, 1994.

Drucker, Peter F. *Innovation and Entrepreneurship.* New York: Harper & Row, 1985.

Edwards, Betty. *Drawing on the Artist Within.* New York: Simon & Schuster, 1986.

———. *Drawing on the Right Side of the Brain.* Rev. ed. New York: G. P. Putnam's Sons, 1989.

Forbes, Cheryl. *Imagination: Embracing a Theology of Wonder.* Portland, Oreg.: Multnomah Press, 1986.

Gaebelein, Frank E. *The Christian, the Arts, and Truth.* Edited by D. Bruce Lockerbie. Portland, Oreg.: Multnomah Press, 1985.

Gardner, Howard. *Creating Minds.* New York: Basic Books, 1993.

———. *Extraordinary Minds.* New York: Basic Books, 1997.

Hall, Doug. *Jump Start Your Brain.* New York: Warner Books, 1995.

Goleman, Daniel, Paul Kaufman, and Michael Ray. *The Creative Spirit.* New York: E. P. Dutton & Co., 1992.

Greene, Katherine, and Richard Greene. *The Man behind the Magic: The Story of Walt Disney.* New York: Viking-Penguin, 1991.

Howard, Pierce J. *The Owner's Manual for the Brain.* Austin, Tex.: Leornian Press, 1994.

Kriegel, Robert J., and Louis Patler. *If It Ain't Broke . . . Break It!!* New York: Warner Books, 1991.

Le Boeuf, Michael. *Imagineering.* New York: Beckley Books, 1980.

LeFever, Marlene D. *Creative Teaching Methods.* Elgin, Ill.: David C. Cook Publishing Co., 1985.

McCullough, Donald W. *The Trivialization of God.* Colorado Springs: NavPress, 1995.

McGee-Cooper, Ann. *You Don't Have to Go Home from Work Exhausted!* New York: Bantam Books, 1992.

Michalko, Michael. *Tinkertoys.* Berkeley, Calif.: Ten Speed Press, 1991.

Nouwen, Henri. *Creative Ministry.* New York: Doubleday & Co., 1971.

O'Connor, Elizabeth. *Eighth Day of Creation.* Waco, Tex.: Word Books, 1971.

Osborn, Alex F. *Applied Imagination.*3d ed. New York: Charles Scribner's Sons, 1979.

Parnes, Sidney J., Ruth B. Noller, and Angelo M Biondi. *Guide to Creative Action.* Rev. ed. New York: Charles Scribner's Sons, 1972.

Peters, Tom. *The Circle of Innovation.* New York: Alfred A. Knopf, 1997.

Peterson, Eugene H. *Traveling Light.* Colorado Springs: Helmers & Howard, 1988.

Postman, Neil. *Amusing Ourselves to Death.* New York: Viking-Penguin, 1985.

Raudsepp, Eugene, with George P. Hough, Jr. *Creative Growth Games.* New York: G. P. Putnam's Sons, 1977.

Ryken, Leland. *Culture in Christian Perspective.* Portland, Oreg.: Multnomah Press, 1986.

Thompson, Charles. *What a Great Idea!* New York: HarperCollins, 1992.

von Oech, Roger. *A Whack on the Side of the Head.* New York: Warner Books, 1983.

———. *A Kick in the Seat of the Pants.* New York: Harper & Row, 1986.

Yancey, Philip. *The Jesus I Never Knew.* Grand Rapids: Zondervan Publishing House, 1995.

Additional Resources

Alden B. Dow Creativity Center, 3225 Cook Road, Midland, MN
48640-2398
Tel: 517-837-4478
Fax: 517-837-4468

The Alden B. Dow Creativity Center is part of Northwood University.
Its purpose is to encourage creativity in individuals. The Center main-
tains a library of books, tapes, and games on the topic of creativity. In
addition, they conduct creativity-related workshops and seminars. They
are the host to the National Conference on Creativity in American
Colleges & Universities.

American Creativity Association, 367 Skyline Orchard Drive,
Hockessin, DE 19707
Tel: 302-239-7673
Fax: 302-234-2840
E-mail: ACA_Moyer@aol.com

ACA is a nonprofit corporation dedicated to the development of
personal and professional creativity. They are a source for books,
educational materials, and conferences.

Buffalo State College, 1300 Elmwood Avenue, Buffalo, NY 14222-1095
Tel: 716-878-6223
Fax: 716-878-4040
Website: www.snybuf.edu/creative/cschp.htm

BSC, part of the State University of New York, offers a Center for Studies in Creativity. Its purpose is to promote and improve understanding of creativity and its many applications. Primarily a degree-granting institution, it advertises the largest creativity library in the world. Known as the Creative Studies Special Collection, the library provides resources to interested individuals and groups. The college also publishes the International Creativity Network Newsletter.

Center for Creative Leadership, One Leadership Place, P.O. Box 26300, Greensboro, NC 27483-6300
Tel: 910-288-7210
Fax: 910-288-3999
E-mail: info@leaders.ccl.org
Website: www.ccl.org

CCL is a nonprofit corporation focused on creativity and leadership, featuring publication and seminars. CCL is also involved in research of leadership and leadership development.

Creative Education Foundation, 1050 Union Road, Buffalo, NY 14224
Tel: 716-675-3181
Fax: 716-675-3209
E-mail: cefhq@cef-cpsi.org
Website: www.cef-cpsi.org

CEF is a nonprofit corporation focused on organizational creativity and problem-solving. CEF produces books, videos, audiotapes, and periodicals related to various aspects of creativity, such as problem-solving, the creative process, education, and leadership. CEF publishes the *Journal of*

Creative Behavior.
Creative Think, P.O. Box 7354, Menlo Park, CA 94026
Tel: 415-321-6775
Fax: 415-321-0609
E-mail: 72234.2450@compuserve.com

Creative Think is a company offering seminars and programs devoted to teaching how to stimulate creative thinking and innovation.

Creative Thinking Association of America, 16600 Sprague Road, Suite 120, Cleveland, OH 44130
Tel: 800-535-0030
Fax: 216-243-8754

This organization offers seminars and workshops designed to stimulate creative thinking. Although primarily a consulting organization, they do offer a small selection of books and tapes related to creativity.

Herrmann International, 794 Buffalo Creek Road, Lake Lure, NC 28746
Tel: 800-432-4234
Fax: 704-625-1402
E-mail: thinking@hbdi.com
Website: www.hbdi.com

Herrmann International offers literature and seminars to stimulate the thinking process. In addition, it offers assessment of thinking styles. The company focuses on applied creative teaching and learning, communication, problem-solving, managing creative people, and developing a climate for stimulating creativity.

Jossey-Bass/Pfeiffer, 350 Sansome Street, San Francisco, CA 94104
Tel: 800-274-4434
Fax: 800-569-0443

Ask for their excellent catalog on training books, activities, and games.
The McNeillis Company, 100 Eighth Avenue, P.O. Box 582, New
Brighton, PA 15066.
Tel: 800-569-6015
Fax: 412-847-9275

This company, using primarily a storyboarding technique, is a source
for long-range creative planning. They have experience working with
churches in various areas, including small-group ministry, various
outreach and age-group ministries, and organization/communication
issues.

Music Works International, P.O. Box 395, Franklin, TN 37065
Tel: 615-591-0001
Fax: 615-591-4369
E-mail: AWENet@aol.com

THINK: The Magazine on Critical and Creative Thinking. Published
by ECS Learning Systems, P.O. Box 701437, San Antonio, TX 78279

Roger von Oech, Creative Think, Box 7354, Menlo Park, CA 94026
Tel: 415-321-6775
Fax: 415-321-0609

The author of the classic *A Whack on the Side of the Head* offers a
number of related resources. His *Creative Whack Pack* is a set of sixty-
four cards, each with a creative exercise or strategy. He describes this as
a "Creativity tool, 'workshop in a box,' oracle, mind-jogger, and a
coach." There is also an electronic version of this tool.

University Associates, 3505 North Campbell Avenue, Suite 505, Tucson,
AZ 85719
Tel: 520-322-6700
Fax: 520-322-6789
E-mail: info@universityassociates.com

Website: www.universityassociates.com
This company focuses primarily on human resource development within organizations. However, it is also a source for books, videos, audiotapes, and periodicals related to various aspects of creativity, such as problem-solving, team games and activities, the creative process, education, and leadership.

WORDplay & Associates, 2016 Woodview Drive, Mount Prospect, IL 60056
Tel: 847-827-9212
Fax: 847-827-6217
E-mail: wordplayassoc@msn.com

This company specializes in workshops designed to foster and increase creativity in individuals and organizations. They use a variety of techniques, including interactive programs and gaming exercises to reduce communication barriers and increase creative potential.

Internet Creativity Resources

> **Creativity Web:** www.ozemail.com.au/~caveman/Creative
> This site offers a variety of resources for creative thinking and also provides a review of software for creativity and idea generation at www.ozemail.com.au/~caveman/Creative/Software/windex.htm.

> **Creativity Internet Resources:** www.waterw.com/~lucia_awlinks.htm.
> **Jossey-Bass Publishers:** www. jbp.com
> Leadership and gaming resources.

> **Simile II:** www.stsintl.com
> Catalog of simulation games.

Answers to Exercises

1. a. 10. This is a simple mathematical (left-brain) progression (n+2).
   b. The sequence is based on rhyming (a right-brain function); therefore use any word that rhymes with show—e.g. row, throw, blow, go, no, etc.
   c. 63. This is another example of a mathematical (left-brain) sequence, based on the formula (nx2) +1.
   d. Red. These are the colors of the spectrum. Interestingly, there are several ways to arrive at this answer. An analytical person (using left-brain thinking) might study the sequence in light of known facts about the relation of these colors to each other and deduce that they represent the colors of the spectrum. By contrast, a more right-brained person might visualize these colors in his mind and recognize the spectrum. Still another person might recall the answer from having memorized the colors of the spectrum.

   If you struggled for a while with this one, you may have been stuck in linear (left-brain) thinking. But this sequence requires more intuitive, nonrational (right-brain) thinking—the kind of thinking that poets tend to use. Here, there is no one "right" answer. The sequence can be completed with more than one word or expression. Consider these answers: fish; a waterfall; mist.

    f. Any word will do! This is a case of pure word association. Where does *your* creative mind take you next?

2. There are at least a couple of answers to this one. Did you get them both?

$$5 + 5 + 5 \neq 550$$

$$5 + 5 + 5 = 550$$

3. Here is a solution to this brain teaser:

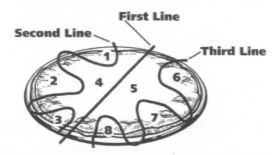

    If you didn't think of slicing the pizza this way, was it because you limited yourself to assuming that the three lines had to be straight lines?

4. 1. He's beside himself

    2. Downtown

    3. Tricycle

    4. Paradise

    5. Long underwear

    6. Neon light

    7. Backwards glance

    8. Paradigms

The Nine Dot Exercise: (Page 107)

The most common mistake made in attempting to solve this problem is to assume that the four lines must remain within the square area created by the dots. But nothing in the instructions forces this limitation. By freeing oneself to draw outside the perimeter, it is possible to find at least two solutions, one of which is shown below. Can you find the other one on your own?

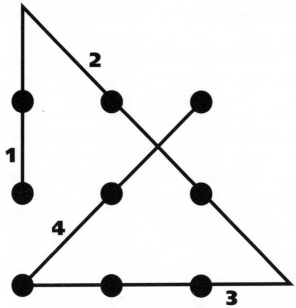

The Sixteen Books of the Bible (Page144)

Here is a list of 15 of the books hidden in the paragraph:

Numbers

Judges

Ruth

Kings

Esther

Job

Lamentations

Mark

Luke

Acts

Titus

Hebrews

James

Peter

Revelation

See if you can locate these books on your own before looking at the paragraph below, where they are shown in **boldface type**.

(Sorry, you'll have to find the sixteenth on your own!)

I once made a re**mark** about the hidden books of the Bible. It was a lu**lu**. **K**e**pt** people loo**king s**o hard for **facts** and for others it was a **revelation**. Some were in a **jam, es**pecially since the names of the books were not capitalized: but the **truth** finally struck home to **numbers** of readers. To others it was a real **job**. We want it to be a most fascinating few moments for you. **YES, THER**E WILL BE SOME REALLY EASY ONES TO SPOT. Others may require **judges** to help them. I will quickly admi**t it us**ually takes a minister to find one of them, and there will be loud **lamentations** when it is found. A little lady says **she brews** a cup of tea so she can concentrate better. See how well you can com**pete. R**elax now, for there are really sixteen names of the books of the Bible in this story.

How Many Squares? (Page 145)

This is tricky! Perhaps you came up with the answer of 26, based on the following method of counting:

16	individual squares
5	squares of 4 units
4	squares of 9 units
1	square of 16 units
26	squares total

Not bad. But your solution reveals a basic assumption that is flawed, from the standpoint of creativity: You have assumed that the diagram is two-dimensional. But what if it's three dimensional and you are merely looking at the object from the end? In that case, there could be an *infinite* number of squares!

Never trust your eyes alone! Creativity demands all of your senses—and *both* sides of your brain!

Scripture Index

Subject Index